More Steam Up!
A Railwayman Remembers

by

Frank Ferneyhough

Foreword by
ALAN PEGLER

ROBERT HALE · LONDON

ISBN 0 7090 2740 0

Robert Hale Limited
Clerkenwell House
Clerkenwell Green
London EC1R 0HT

British Library Cataloguing in Publication Data

Ferneyhough, Frank
   More steam up!:   a railwayman remembers.
   1. Ferneyhough, Frank   2. British Rail
   — Biography
   I. Title
   385'.092'4   HE3018.2F4

ISBN 0-7090-2740-9

Photoset in North Wales by
Derek Doyle & Associates, Mold, Clwyd
Printed in Great Britain by
St Edmundsbury Press, Bury St Edmunds, Suffolk
Bound by Hunter & Foulis Ltd

Contents

Illustrations

CREDITS

Permission to reproduce illustrations has been granted by the following: British Rail, 6, 7, 8, 13, 18, 22, 24-5, 28, 31, 33-6, 39, 44; John Dixon, 38; H. Guest, 20; Terry Nicholls, 2; R. Palmer, 10; Allan Robey V.O.R.R.S.A., 1; Science Museum, 12, 27; James Hall Thomson, 40-1; Venice Simplon-Orient-Express, 19; Wayland Picture Library, 5, 23; P. Winding, 9. A few illustrations of unknown source are believed to be free of copyright, but the author, c/o the publishers, would be pleased to correspond with any claimant.

Acknowledgements

For the author it is a pleasure as well as an obligation to acknowledge with gratitude the generous help and advice he has received from many friends and former colleagues, including John Hughes, Philip Wilson, Alex Murray, Richard Saunderson, George Wilde, Frances Heckler, Bob Townsend and Felix Slade. He also thanks most warmly those countless railwaymen down the line and over the years who made life in steam railways so varied, venturesome and happy. He gladly acknowledges, too, the splendid work done for the preservation of steam railways by the many societies under the leadership of Peter Manisty. And finally he thanks his wife, Joan, for help with proof-reading, and her discerning literary eye for awkward syntax, a split infinitive and a hung participle.

Dedication:
For my wife, Joan,
and Roger, Hilary
and Stephen

Foreword

by Alan Pegler, Fellow Royal Society of Arts; president, Festiniog Railway Company and Society; former member, British Railways Eastern Region Board; one-time owner of the world-famous *Flying Scotsman*.

Talk abounds today about things going full circle. Activities and interests fashionable years ago become popular again. Currently there is a tremendous feel for how things were years ago: for example, steam trains. Interest grows yearly – over two million enthusiasts, five hundred railway societies, five hundred assorted preserved locomotives. Incredibly, in 1963 only one express steam locomotive in private ownership was allowed to run on British Rail tracks – good old 4472 *Flying Scotsman*. What a wonderful ambassador it became! Thanks to its vast publicity, other steam-locomotives were saved or resurrected from scrapping. Today between forty and fifty are allowed to haul enthusiasts' specials on BR tracks.

At the 150th anniversary celebrations of the Liverpool & Manchester Railway staged at Rainhill in 1980, Frank Ferneyhough and I worked closely together, and I found his book about that railway most valuable for my broadcast commentaries there. We also worked alongside for a while for the Venice Simplon-Orient-Express: I in various capacities and he as the historical writer.

Losing steam in the 1960s may have saddened Frank, but he is a realist. He knows that change is inevitable. But in his new book his delightful cameos of the years when steam was king provide laughter and tears and reveal the fun ordinary railwaymen had in their daily work, and simultaneously give an insight behind the scenes – at stations and goods depots, in signalboxes and control rooms, at marshalling yards and on the track.

His latest effort is refreshing, highly entertaining, fast moving, easy to read. Once the proofs were in my hands, I found them hard to put down. Frank's book, his ninth, again displays his talents as an accomplished and engaging raconteur in a narrative that is laced liberally with amusing anecdotes and – yes – nostalgia. I loved it. I am sure you will too.

Alan Tyler.

1

The Magic of Steam for the Young

I was more than anxious. I was definitely alarmed. As the steam train rattled along on the metals, the rhythmic clank-clank we could hear beneath the carriage was growing louder. Could it really denote danger? Again I glanced up at the communication cord, and it seemed to hold me spellbound. David Cave and Jack Podmore, two fellow railway clerks, all of us aged nineteen, stared at me, fear darkening their eyes.

Jack urged, 'Pull it, Frank! For heaven's sake, pull it!'

'Why me?'

David chipped in: 'Go on! You're the oldest.'

At that time we all worked temporarily in the railway headquarters offices at Derby and were travelling on our regular morning train from Stoke-on-Trent. Now it was between Uttoxeter and Sudbury and, because it was non-corridor stock, we couldn't reach the guard.

Louder and more urgent grew the clanking. Looking at each other, we all rose to our feet. If we pulled the cord and delayed the train, we might be in trouble with our bosses at Derby. But if we didn't and the train was really in danger, we might not even get to Derby to tell the tale.

A particularly loud clank settled it. I grabbed the cord and pulled it hard. Immediately the train began to slow down. 'You've done it now, Ferney, old lad!' said Jack.

Trembling all over, I sat down suddenly, as Jack and David broke into hysterical laughter. Just as abruptly, they stopped and sat down too. The scenery was passing more slowly now, but there was no sign of the train actually stopping. Unknown to me then, the cord gave only a partial braking, leaving the driver free to run conveniently to the next station.

A somewhat subdued David remarked. 'We'll be late for work.'

'Worse than that,' added Jack. 'Frank'll have to pay the penalty. £5 for improper use!'

But having done the deed, I was feeling a little more relaxed now. 'Gosh, that's my wages for 2½ weeks,' I cracked.

Soon we were running into Sudbury station and the butterflies returned. I stepped down onto the platform to await the guard. Sure enough, he came striding along, red in the face. 'Who the bloody hell did that? Oh, it's you, young Ferneyhough. What are you playing at, eh?'

It was Mr Greaves, a friend of my father's. Bending low, I looked under the carriage, saw an iron rod hanging awkwardly loose and pointed it out. Mr Greaves stooped to take a look. 'Oh, I see. That loose rod. Looks as though it's broken off the dynamo. I'll try and fix it.' (The dynamo was belt-driven from a wheel-axle and provided the lighting for the carriage.) He walked to his van and returned with a piece of strong cord. Meantime the stationmaster appeared and many passengers had alighted from the train to see what was afoot.

David whispered mischievously in my ear, 'Let's hope no other train bashes into the back of ours!'

'Don't be so darned cheerful, Dave!'

Having done a running repair, Mr Greaves blew his whistle, and the passengers scrambled quickly into the train. As I entered my compartment again, he called to me. 'Don't worry, lad. You did the right thing. See your boss when you gets to Derby.'

'Thanks, Mr Greaves. I'll do that.'

'That dynamo would have fell off afore long. Could a-been real trouble, lad.' He waved his flag and the train steamed off.

We reached our office half an hour late, and I reported to the chief clerk. Surprisingly he smiled and told me not to worry about it. He had already heard the details by telephone.

When the panic was over, I had to admit to a secret pleasure at having halted a main-line train. Very few railway people, I thought, would ever have done it. Certainly it

would be something to talk about for many years to come.
A month after the incident, I received written compliments from my boss plus a postal order for £1, which was equivalent to more than half a week's wages.

How does an ordinarily sensible chap like me get caught up in this mad, crazy desire to make a life for himself among the steam trains? An actor or a singer, yes. A racing driver or a mountain-climber, perhaps. A jockey, a joiner, a tightrope-walker, maybe. But all these seemed to be such boring old jobs compared with working on a railway station.

When we are young, we most of us have wonderful dreams about the great future we are going to carve for ourselves. How marvellous to achieve your ambitions and then, in later life, be able to look back on all the ups and downs with the pride and joy of deep and lasting satisfaction.

So often, Lady Luck will throw the dice. Much depends upon the accident of where you were born and brought up. I was born on the edge of Hanley, one of the five towns of Stoke-on-Trent in north Staffordshire, immortalized by our own home-grown author, Arnold Bennett. We lived about fifty yards from the railway branch line that ran for a dozen miles between Stoke and Leek. During the day and sometimes in the night, inside the house or out, we could hear the trains, passenger and goods, chuff-chuffing away and sometimes sounding their whistles. And at night, when the fireman opened the furnace doors to stoke up the fire, the bright glow lit up the sky as though from a forest fire. In my cradle days I was surely rocked to sleep to the regular rhythm of the passing steam trains.

As soon as I was big enough, I would hurry across the road and stand by the iron fence to watch the trains go by. Sometimes the driver or the fireman would smile and wave. For me, the smell of warm oil and steam was most exciting, and even the occasional smut in the eye was part of the natural phenomena.

On our way to the infants' school which I attended up to the age of seven, we kids passed beneath a railway bridge and had the frightening thrill of being under it as a train thundered over the top. Later, on the way to the 'big school', we passed *over* a bridge. Often we were tempted to lean over the parapet to catch a can of steam in a cocoa tin. Sometimes a frightened boy would accidentally let go of his tin, and it would drop onto the engine. Then he would run like mad to get away as fast as possible from the scene of the crime.

A hundred yards along the line, near Bucknall station, was a shunting yard of several sidings. It was spanned by a public footbridge. We spent hours on that bridge, just watching engines pushing and shoving the wagons from one siding to another. The pattern of movement was a farrago of mystery to be understood only by the shunters busy with their coupling-poles, whistles and hand signals. It was quite beyond the perception of our youthful intellects. One day, all would be revealed to me.

We ventured on the footbridge in all seasons. Whether in the deep snow of January or the blazing heat of July, the sidings were always entrancing. When we stood directly over a passing engine, we could feel the warm steam up the legs of our short trousers and would run and jump about, squealing with delight.

So I grew up with the familiar sight of railwaymen going to and from their work at unusual hours of the day, unlike the factory workers in the potteries who had a regular day shift. Besides, the railwaymen wore smart uniforms, and they wore proudly on their caps a badge with the letters 'NSR'. Later I was to learn that this stood for the North Staffordshire Railway, a small but valiant company that in 1923 was to be gobbled up by the voracious jaws of that great monster the LMS Railway Company.

One man I frequently saw was a driver. He wore a boilersuit of blue overalls and a black jacket, with his peaked cap well over his left ear. He had the biggest moustache I had ever seen, and it was bright ginger. He seemed to lift it up to get his pipe into his mouth. Mr Turner walked along our road on the way to nearby Bucknall station to catch a train to Stoke, over two miles distant. Whenever I passed him, I made it my business to say, 'How d'you do', like the other men in the road. Though I was only ten, I wanted him to realize that I was growing up and old enough to have a ride on his engine down at the Stoke engine-sheds. An inspector at Stoke station had let me into the driver's cab in Stoke station a year ago, when my Dad took me there. So that was a good start.

In the road one day I stopped him. 'How d'you do, Mr Turner.'

'Hallo, son. What do thee want, eh?'

'A ride on your engine, please!'

He roared with laughter as I walked beside him. Then he became serious.

'Tell thee what, lad. It be Sunday tomorrer. Can you come wi' me in the afternoon? We wunna be very busy, and there won't be no bosses about.'

I went with him on the half past two train from Bucknall station. Then at Stoke we walked down the slope at the end of the platform and into the loco yard. Mr Turner held my hand firmly. A couple of engines stood in the yard, small puffs of steam escaping with arrogant prodigality from the chimney and from various pipes at the side. He found a rough form for me to sit on, instructing me not to move, while he vanished somewhere into the mysterious depths of the engine shed where several engines, large and small, were standing. On his return, he took me to a shunting engine where his fireman was already in the driving-cab. He helped me up to the footplate – the floor of the driving-cab – and Mr Turner told him, 'This lad, he wants to work on the railway.'

'Right, boy. You can 'ave my job any day o' the wick!'

Mr Turner gave me a piece of rag. 'Hold on to this 'ere pipe. But it's hot. So keep your cloth in your hand.'

The fireman had been shovelling coal into the firebox, and the bright glow from the roaring furnace lit up his sweating face. He closed the firebox doors with a clatter of metal against metal, and the driver began to move his engine slowly, with steady chuff-chuffs from the chimney, to the other end of the engine shed. He stopped, turned his reversing-handle and came back gently from where we had started. It didn't take very long. But I can't tell you how

exciting it was at ten years old, to be up there on a real live
steam-engine, to sense it rumbling beneath your feet, to feel
the heat from the fire and to be actually on the move.
I think it was at that moment that I was hooked. I just had
to work on the railway. And I didn't care where. It could be
on the engines, on the track, at a station or even in the
offices.

One morning I was standing with some other boys by the
iron fencing alongside the railway. We were watching for
the morning goods train and stood about fifty yards from the
railway bridge that crossed the River Trent. Sydney Austin
had collected some small pieces of wood, so I asked him,
'What d'you want them for?'

'Chuck at the train, you fool!'

I wanted to say, 'Don't be so daft,' but he was bigger than
me. He was always bullying little chaps. In the distance we
heard the throbbing and thrusting of the train. As the engine
came almost level with us, travelling slowly, Sydney threw a
piece of wood towards it, then flung another. The fireman
was playing a hose onto the coal bunker, to keep the coal
dust down, I suppose. Quick as a flash, he turned the hose
on the boy and soaked him to the skin. How we laughed at
him as he ran off home leaving a trail of wet footprints
behind him. The next day we were amazed to hear that he
had told his mother that some big boys had pushed him into
the Trent.

When I reached eleven years, the headmaster, Mr Pennell,
said, 'Talk to your father about going to the High School.'

I did. My Dad, head gardener at a hospital, told me,
'Maybe I could send one, but I couldn't send the other three.'

It was a good school, Bucknall Council School. An
elementary school. Three hundred and fifty boys and girls
between seven and fourteen. Over fifty in each class. Our
dedicated teachers were smartly dressed and maintained
strong but fair discipline. At twelve, I was placed in a small
experimental studies group, and we added to our normal
subjects Pitman's shorthand, French, Latin roots and
algebra. My hobby, reading, nourished by Frank Richards'
captivating schoolboy weeklies, *Magnet* and *Gem*, was

maturing splendidly in the literary idiom of young boys, towards Biggles and Sexton Blake.

I left school at fourteen. The headmaster gave me a good report and recommended me for clerical work, but the best my Dad could find for me at that time was a job as a butcher's boy, which I did for two years. Then, in 1927, a friend of my father, a railway inspector, tried to get me on the railway. I was sent by train to the LMS headquarters at Derby, nearly forty miles distant, where I took a clerical and a medical examination. There was great excitement in the household when, a few days later, a letter arrived from Derby instructing me officially to start at Hanley station in the parcels department as a junior clerk. I had attained my ambition.

The work was to do with the despatch of packages of merchandise of all kinds to all parts of Britain. Some of the packages were brought into the station by our horse parcels vans, others by firms' vehicles or by private individuals. And there was the delivery of in-coming merchandise around the town, also by our two horse-drawn vans. Mr Payne, the stationmaster, had six or seven clerks on his staff, including a chief clerk, also two station foremen, some shunters, two ticket-collectors, two vanmen, two vanboys, several porters and a few signalmen.

All the work was new to me, and I found it hard going at first, working out the charges for parcels, collecting the money, sending out accounts to customers, coping with the paperwork such as delivery sheets and consignment notes. But my colleagues were most patient and helpful. It was exciting to feel part of a busy railway station with trains running in and out all day, the bustle of the parcels office with masses of packages of all kinds going through, some to send away, others coming in off a train. There was fun with some of the customers. Our cloakroom was used by commercial travellers and by stage people from the two theatres in the town. And the trams' whining, warning bells sounding, wheels squealing on the tramlines up and down the nearby road all day.

Yes, I think I am going to be happy here. It did occur to me that one day I might eventually rise to be a stationmaster, but I never expected that I should reach that level in ten years and reach middle management level at London headquarters with my own private office and first-class railway travel within a further ten.

Meanwhile, setbacks were certain to come my way, but I was to have much fun on the way up.

2
Goats, a Frog and Day-old Chicks

In the parcels office we handled all sorts of livestock, cats, dogs, pigeons, chicks, cockerels, maggots, snakes, guinea-pigs, anything. Jack Merrill, the parcels porter, fortyish, smart in his neat uniform, came into the parcels office from the station platform. In his hand was a length of strong cord. At the other end was a large goat. It had huge horns and a powerful baa-aa-aa which made unsuspecting customers jump in surprise.

In the office were Mr Grocott, the chief clerk, and another porter. One of the customers, a lad about my age, simply rocked with laughter. Cheekily he said to Jack, 'Is that your pet, or is he going to Blackpool for his holidays?'

With that, he gave the goat a playful pat on his broad and bony back. In fright, the goat jumped and snatched the cord from Jack's tight grip. Jack tried to catch the animal, which was now trotting round the parcels office, making goat noises and leaving on the floor visual evidence of his fright.

Finally Jack grabbed his horns, grasped the cord and tied him to a hook on the doorpost. Glaring at the youth, now embarrassed, he growled, 'You silly young idiot!' To Mr Grocott he commented, 'No label on him. But the label string's here on his collar. He must have eaten it.'

'Right, Jack. We'll phone Stoke and Congleton for a start, and see if we can trace anything.'

Meanwhile the goat was still restless. Suddenly he lowered his head, made a fearsome charge at the youth's posterior and sent him sprawling into piles of wooden boxes. He was somewhat bruised and shaken. As he helped the boy to his feet, Jack grinned, 'That's your comeuppance, me lad. So don't you play the giddy goat again!'

The lad finished his business in the office and mooched off quietly, rubbing his bottom.

Using the piece of cord, Jack had tied up the goat afresh to the leg of a large desk. We hadn't noticed how close he was to some day-old chicks chirruping away in a carton standing on a barrow. But notice we did when two or three of the chicks were suddenly found running around the parcels office floor. Mr Grocott hurried to the scene, his grey moustache bristling with anxiety.

'Close that door! Don't let them get out or we'll have a claim on our hands!'

He picked up the carton, put his hand over the hole that had been chewed by the goat, then plastered a piece of strong sticky paper over it to keep the other chicks in, as a temporary measure.

Jack and I were chasing a chirping chick each around the parcels on the floor, and in and out of all sorts of nooks and crannies we never knew existed. A few customers waiting in the office joined in the fun of chick-catching. Jack and I caught one each and held their warm little bodies cupped in our hands. Mr Grocott was still busy chasing his quarry, but the tiny bundle of yellow fluff kept eluding him. Then he bravely changed his battle tactics. He took off his bowler hat, bent down and tried to pop it over the chick. But the chick didn't like this at all. He was a surprisingly quick chick, and agile for one so young.

Poor Mr Grocott stumbled over a half gallon of cream that had arrived off the last train, from one of the big dairies, went his length and badly bashed his precious bowler hat. Meanwhile one of the customers in the chick chase caught the truant and offered it to the chief clerk. Mr Grocott held out his bowler hat. 'Put it in there, sir,' and carefully he placed his hand over the chick to stop it hopping out.

Jack had found a small wooden box where two of the chicks were already ensconced, and Mr Grocott gently lifted his little truant from his hat and placed it with the other two. Lovingly he brushed his hat with his hand and pushed out the dents. He was about to put it on his head when he swore under his breath, 'The dirty little bugger. Just look at what he's done in my hat!'

Jack Merrill and I fell about laughing. Even the customers chortled. When peace was restored and Mr Grocott had resumed his usual *savoir faire*, Jack said to him, 'You said "he". But "he" is a "she".'

'How do you know that, Jack?'

'They're for egg-laying later on.'

'Then she ought to know better!'

Shortly after, the customer, whom we had telephoned, came to collect the chicks, and Mr Grocott had to explain and to apologize for the goat's unwelcome behaviour. He was about to return to his inner office when he heard Jack shout angrily, 'Get out of it, you beast!'

The can of cream that had tripped Mr Grocott was now leaking, and the goat was enjoying a culinary delight that happy chance had brought his way. His great brown eyes sparkled and thick cream dripped down his beard. Jack grabbed the cord and tied it up to be shorter, to separate the animal from the cream. Billygoat Gruff was not at all pleased and gave him a baleful glare.

Mr Grocott wasn't too pleased either, though for a different reason. He picked up the can of cream and took it to his inner office, saying to Jack, 'We're certain to have a claim about this lot.'

When Mr Grocott was out of earshot, I said, 'Tell me, honestly, Jack. Do you like goats?'

'No I don't. I hate the bloody things, and they stink!'

'Do you like poetry then?'

He grinned. 'No, not me. I doesn't understand the stuff.'

'I've got a poem at home that's got a link with your work. I think you'll enjoy it.'

'I doubts it.' Then he chuckled. 'I'm illegitimate.'

'Oh, d'you mean illiterate?'

'No. Both, you silly bugger!' He guffawed at that.

Next day I accosted Jack when things were quiet. 'That poem. I've got it. My uncle says it dates from the 1890s.'

Taking the sheet of paper, Jack sat down on a crate and read slowly. When he had finished, his face lit up. 'Eh, young Ferney. You've changed my life.'

'How d'you mean?'

'This poetry business. You've bin and got me 'ooked!'

I returned the faded sheet to my pocket. It read:

The Goat's Dilemma.

A red shirt hung upon the line,
A goat came along and thought t'was fine;
He took a hold and chewed it down,
And swallowed it without a frown.

The man came forth with hue and cry,
He then declared the goat must die.
He threw him down upon his back
And tied him to the railway track.

He waited long to see the smoke,
And hear the engine's steady stroke.
And when he did he grinned and said,
'Mr Goat, you'll soon be dead!'

The train came on with deafening shriek,
Which made the goat feel pretty weak.
He gave one awful mighty strain,
Threw up the shirt and stopped the train!

So much for goats. Horses are much more interesting. I used to see much of our two parcels van horses, Captain and Blossom. They were stabled overnight along with the horses serving the nearby goods department. Goods horses hauled flat drays that carried a wide range of merchandise, from barrels of beer from Burton-on-Trent and sacks of grain from farmers, to machinery parts and manufactured articles.

On my occasional visits to the goods office, I often longed to ride one of those great shire horses bareback. They were just beautiful animals; gentle giants, one of the stablemen called them. Large they might be, but they were the most lovable and affectionate creatures you could imagine. There was a black one, a white one, some fine dapple greys and splendid chestnuts, with massive manes, fetlocks that flopped around their feet as the animal plodded around the town's streets, and rich tails that in the heat of the summer could flick the flies off with a deadly swish. Of course, railway horses were not the only ones that plied the town. There were more horse-drawn vehicles than motor lorries doing both town and country work.

Great care was taken by the railway managements of their valued equestrian teams, under the supervision of their own veterinary surgeons. The LMS issued a booklet for carters and stablemen with up-to-date instructions. Page 1 begins: 'Don't jerk or tug the reins all the time; it is bad driving, spoils the horse's mouth and doesn't make him work any better. Don't hit your horse across the nose; it makes him nervous and may make him vicious as well. Don't lose your temper with your horse; it is unsportsmanlike. Don't try to turn the horse too quickly or in a small space for this may cause him to tread one foot over the other with painful consequences.'

'Remember,' says the booklet, 'that almost any horse will do his best for his driver, and that your horse knows whether you are a good driver or not. All horses are very nervous, and some horses are rather stupid.' No teasing, says the booklet, especially addressed to cart-boys, for this tends to make them vicious.

Food and drink? 'When at work, horses are to be given not less than three feeds daily and two on Sundays, and to be watered at least three times daily ... Smoking in stables is strictly prohibited.' (We can't have our railway horses getting bad habits from their human masters.)

What about bedtime? 'Bedding must be spread over the floor of the stall to such an extent that the horse's hindquarters are not on the bare floor when lying down.' (Nothing is said about reading Dobbin a bedtime story.)

And here is an instruction aimed at people who fancy a joyride on a dappled grey shire: 'No carter or other servant of the Company is allowed to use the Company's horse ... for any purpose whatsoever other than that relating to the Company's business ... Carters are reminded to obtain lamps for vehicles if there is a likelihood of their being away from the station after lighting-up time.' Such lamps were normally lit by oil.

No one was allowed to ride on the vehicle except the carter and cart-boy or attendant – which calls to mind the rides my friend Cliff Dutton and I used to have each Monday morning on the way to school. The empty flat dray was on its way to a farm at Milton to collect bags of potatoes. The first Monday we walked behind the dray holding on with our hands, but the driver called out, 'Come up front alonga me, lads.' It was a real treat to sit up there behind that fine horse and to catch a whiff of his sweating body on the breeze. Occasionally the drayman would tap his hindquarters with his whip. Not that it made a scrap of difference to the horse's plodding clip-clop pace.

Back to the booklet. One section is headed 'Securing and protecting the traffic'. As with many other words, 'traffic' in railwayese covers everything the railways carry, from passengers and live animals to machinery and loads of coal. 'Traffic' falls into one of two groups – passenger traffic conveyed by passenger train, and goods traffic conveyed by goods train. There is a whole series of words which the railways have adopted and adapted to their own special needs for well over a century. A few that come to mind include shunter, coupling, footplate, chair, sleeper, truck, wagon, engine, pilotman, guard, platelayer, fishplate, key, tablet, regulator, coach, trolley, semaphore, sprag, points, junction, guard, gangway, block. In common language, each has several recognizable meanings, but each has only one meaning to railwaymen. So you can see what sort of difficulties we beginners had to face!

Elsewhere in the horse booklet is a heading – 'Learn, give and obey the recognized traffic signals'. It continues, 'On roads where white lines are marked as a guidance to traffic, care must be taken to see that vehicles are kept within the spaces marked off by the lines.' About that time electric traffic lights were beginning to come into general use. The first automatic ones were installed in 1927. Everybody called them 'robots', to rhyme with 'repose'.

Most horse-drivers, for some obscure reason known as 'carmen', were proud of the horsebrasses which they fixed to bridles and to saddles. Once a year the horses were put on show. Brasses were highly polished, saddles rubbed up to a sparkly shine, manes and tails were beautifully plaited and decorated with straw or coloured raffia now almost a lost art. Competitions were held in Hanley goods yard, and railway officials acted as judges and presented winners with modest cash prizes of a few shillings each. One carman with whom I was friendly, Joe Bornley, often won prizes. Back on the streets with his dray, he delighted in showing off his beribboned circular emblem in red which he would fix firmly to his whip.

Selected horses were displayed also on feast days and at annual horse shows customarily held on Easter or Whit Monday. They shared these fêtes with a variety of country activities such as children dancing round the maypole; Morris dancers in their traditional white costume, bells on their ankles, white handkerchiefs to wave, and a concertina or fiddle to dance to; and a brass band. Other attractions would include such exciting adventures as the egg-and-spoon race and the sack race.

The little I knew about horses I learned from my maternal grandfather, who owned a couple of narrowboats which he plied with horsepower on the Trent and Mersey Canal. His stables were close by his cottage a few miles from my home, and he sometimes allowed me, as a small boy, to ride bareback around the nearby lanes.

So at Hanley station I kept hoping for a chance to ride one of the railway shire horses. Nothing ambitious. Just a pleasant amble round the goods yard when there were no bosses about. Joe Bornley, I felt, was my best bet. Whenever I greeted him with 'Hallo, Joe,' he would answer in a friendly way, 'Eh-up, young Jim, what you up to?' He called me Jim because my Dad was named Jim, and they used to drink together at the Finney Gardens pub.

Then one day it happened. I was in the goods yard and saw him leading the handsome Duke from the stables. The other draymen had already gone on their rounds, and the yard was pretty quiet. He greeted me as usual and I told him how much I would like a ride on Duke. He grinned broadly. 'They'd sack me for that, young Jim. Besides, you canna ride an 'oss.'

'Yes I can, Joe. I go on my grandad's.' A legitimate

exaggeration, this, to a desperate seventeen-year-old seeking a modest excitement.

'Tell thee what. Gaffer's going out. See him yonder.'

Sure enough, the goods agent was making briskly for the exit gates. The only activity in the goods yard was that of an 0-6-0 tank-engine shunting in the sidings. As soon as the gaffer was out of sight, Joe looked at me. 'Up you get, then.'

There were no stirrups, of course, but Duke had his blinkers on, his bridle and bit, and short reins, all I needed. I stood on a box to get mounted, and felt his warm flesh under me, my somewhat short legs stretched astride his wide girth.

Joe gave him a smack on the rump. 'Gee-up, Duke!'

And Duke did gee-up, but very gently, clip-clop clip-clop. He wasn't going to put himself out for any whippersnapper of a joyrider on this fresh spring morning. That is, until the shunting engine gave a piercing shriek on its whistle at the very moment that it blew off steam in a very loud buzz that bored fiercely into your hearing-apparatus. Now he suddenly went into a jog-trot, bouncing me up and down on his back. Without stirrups it was not very pleasant, I assure you.

I called to him, 'Easy, Duke. Easy, now' but he began to go faster, and I could hear old Joe running after us and shouting, 'Duke, way, whoa. Whoa there, Duke!' Duke ignored his master too.

When he trotted through the exit of the goods yard and out into the road, I began to feel really panicky, and the butterflies fluttered deep in my stomach. Luckily there wasn't much traffic about, but a tramcar was coming down the road towards us. Passengers stared out of the window. Not at all helpful, the tram-driver began to stamp on the foot pedal that worked his warning bell, and Duke picked up more speed, making a turn in the process. This caused me to lose my reins. I grabbed his heavy mane and hung on for dear life. I found I was slipping to the right. I strained every muscle to stay upright, otherwise I could easily slip right off and fall under Duke's massive feet. By now I was really frightened. Something had to happen soon, and it happened sooner than expected.

A policeman jumped from the tramcar, dashed across the

road, grabbed the reins and gradually brought the excited animal to a halt. He patted the horse's neck affectionately and gently stroked him, talking to him quietly all the time. He was a young policeman, and as he helped me down from the horse, he grinned, 'What are you trying to do, lad, a rodeo act?'

Joe walked up at the same time and roundly ticked me off. Rightly, he was very angry. 'You don't ride no 'oss o' mine no more, young Jim!'

I was shaking and sweating and hung my head awkwardly. 'Sorry, Joe. Very sorry. I won't do it again.'

'Joe, I'll leave you to deal with this youth. It's lucky there wasn't an accident. I won't be making a report.'

Joe was relieved. 'Ta, mate. Ta very much.'

The things Joe said to me as he walked the horse back to the goods yard are too embarrassing for me to relate, and I was worrying about what he might say to my father. As though he read my thoughts, he smiled and winked: 'I'll not be telling your Dad. Not for a wick or so, anyroad!'

We still remained good friends, despite his receiving a sharp letter from the goods agent and my having to apologize to the stationmaster. After all, you can't go rodeo riding around a goods yard without getting a lash from a horsewhip, so to speak, if only by proxy.

Some weeks after my rodeo escapade, a customer came into the parcels office carrying a small wooden box drilled with airholes. A chap about forty, he wore a check cloth cap pulled over on one side, reminding me of the local pigeon-flyers. The box was of thin plywood and carried a warning label, 'This side up.'

I greeted him. 'Good afternoon, sir. I'll put it on the scales. What's in it, please?'

'It's livestock.'

'Right. Is it an animal?'

'No. Just livestock.' He sounded mysterious, and I began to wonder what the blazes it could be. Maybe a snake or something.

'Is it a bird, a pigeon?'

'No, not a bird. Just livestock.'

His evasion was getting me nowhere fast. I needed to know the contents to look up the rate to be charged. We had scores of rates for all kinds of things.

'An animal, then?'

'No!' He really growled. Was this a clue?

'Sorry to bother you, sir, but I need to know what it is, so that I can look up the charge.'

The man fairly spat it out. 'It's a frog!'

'A frog?'

'A frog.'

'I've never had a frog before. Not to send away by train. I'll have to look up the regulations about frogs, to see how much to charge.'

Always helpful and keeping an eye on me, Mr Grocott, the chief clerk, came up. 'Any problems?'

'Not really, Mr Grocott. I'm trying to find a rate for this box. It's livestock.'

'What sort of livestock?'

'A frog.'

His eyebrows shot up. 'A frog?'

'That's what the gentleman says.'

The customer enlarged for our enlightenment. 'It's a thoroughbred, you see.'

'A frog, a thoroughbred?'

'Yes. And it's no good you laughing, me lad. Them thoroughbreds is highly strung.' I thought I heard a little croak.

'Funny,' said Mr Grocott, 'but we've never had a frog before. Not to send away by train.'

Truculently, the customer chipped in. 'What's so funny about a frog? Does you want my business or doesn't you?'

Mr Grocott lifted his curly bowler hat with one hand, and with the other he scratched his head with his dip pen. Soothingly he tried to placate the man.

'Yes, sir. Of course we do. We're just looking in our reference books how to charge for it. Our job here is to help you with your frog.'

With patience, I turned page after page of the regulations. 'Can't see anything under Frog.'

Mr Grocott leaned enquiringly towards the customer. 'Frogs can live on land or in water, can't they?'

'A-course they can.'

To me, the chief clerk said, 'Look under Amphibians.'

I turned more pages. 'Nothing under Amphi-what-you-said.'

Parcels porter Jack Merrill and a couple of customers listened intently but pretended not to.

'Why not try Rodents, Frank.'

Crossly the customer responded, 'It's not a bloody rat. It's a bloody frog!'

The chief coaxed, 'Take it gently, sir.'

'Nothing under Rodents,' I told Mr Grocott.

He suggested, 'Let's try insects.'

This struck me as funny and I began to laugh. The whole business was becoming slightly ludicrous. But our customer was furious. 'It's no laughing matter, lad. And it's not a bloody insect!'

I whispered, 'It can't be under Insects, Mr Grocott.'

'Oh, no. I suppose not. Let's try Reptiles. No luck? I'll tell you what. We'll charge it under the livestock regulations as a puppy in a box.'

'Sounds like a good idea.'

I placed the box on the Avery scales, and it weighed just two pounds. For a moment I thought the customer was going raving mad. He waved his arms about and shouted, to the embarrassment of the other customers, 'It's not a puppy, for Pete's sake. Puppies don't croak. You lot doesn't know your business!' He suddenly grabbed the box, turned on his heel and bellowed. 'I'm taking it up to the Post Office. I might get some sense out of that lot. Good day!'

Such relief after he had gone. Mr Grocott and I looked a little sheepishly at each other, then grinned. I said to him, 'Frogs spawn under water, don't they. And fish do the same. We never looked under Fish.'

The old man chuckled. 'For all I care, he can send it by Pickford's Heavy Haulage and be done with it!'

I smiled at the next customer, who put a suitcase on the counter. 'Can I help you, sir?'

3

They Passed by my Window

My next brief at Hanley station was to be trained in the
mysteries of the ticket booking-office. The very idea scared
me somewhat. Big queues and awkward questions at busy
holiday times and bank holidays. Just suppose a gentleman
comes to the booking-office window and says, 'I want 2½
returns, please, to Gorachwood via Dublin at the cheapest
rate. I want a ticket for my dog and insurance for the journey
including the ship. And I shall want to send my luggage in
advance. Could you tell me how much it will cost, please,
where we have to change, how long we will have to wait at
the changing stations, and is it best to go via Liverpool or
Holyhead or Fleetwood or Heysham, or is there any other
shipping route to Dublin, and what times do the ships leave
the port, please? Sorry to bother you.'
  Phew! This could be coped with in one of several ways:
'Sorry, sir. I'm new here. Why not go to Stoke and book
there? They're expert on Ireland' or 'I'm just closing the
office for lunch' or 'I'm now going off duty' or 'Come back
this afternoon when my colleague will be on duty. He's
better at it than I' or 'Why not go to Blackpool instead?
Marvellous sands there. And a wonderful Punch and Judy
show for your little boy' or, as a last resort, 'Pardon me, sir,
while I have a nervous breakdown.'
  That kind of booking used to give me nightmares. Yet
nothing like it ever happened to me while at Hanley. Which
confirms my growing philosophy that many of our daily
anxieties are about crises, minor or major, which never
happen.
  During the training period of a week or so, I was under
the watchful and helpful eyes of Mr Poole, the middle-aged
chief booking-clerk, and the two booking-clerks, aged about
thirty, who worked early and late shifts alternate weeks.
'Early' was 5 a.m. to 1 p.m. and 'late' 3 p.m. to 11 p.m. While

training I worked a middle shift.

There was the ticket-issuing system to learn, also the book-keeping and the use of the timetables. Other tasks included making up the cash for daily banking at the National Provincial Bank in Hanley, drawing money from the bank to pay the wages of all the staff and compiling the wages bills. At seventeen it was a lot to absorb, I can tell you.

For the run-of-the-mill booking I had no problem. The variety of tickets was limited mainly to ordinary, workmen's and reduced fares for weekend and monthly returns. Reduced fares were also offered to genuine commercial travellers and to groups of theatrical people for their tours. We booked two parties each week for the two theatres in the town that changed their programmes each week. Two classes were available for everybody – first and third.

For me, whatever I was doing, there was always the ambience of the railway station. The sounds were music in my ears. Steam trains in and out of the station all day, goods and passenger. The banging of the carriage doors, the guard's whistle, the engine's siren or whistle, the chatter of passengers getting off the trains and passing the ticket-collector's cabin, the rattle of platform barrows loaded with merchandise, postmen with barrow loads of mailbags. And always there was the smell of warm steam that permeated the station.

An intriguing piece of equipment in the booking-office was the dating-press. Painted black, it was crudely made in cast iron and was invented in the nineteenth century. It stood about nine inches high, was cylindrical in shape and was screwed onto the counter near the booking-office window and in sight of the passengers. Each passenger ticket issued had to have a date imprinted on it. This was done by thrusting it into a gap in the middle of the dating-press and – hey presto! – the date was printed on it by a black inking ribbon. It was also extremely efficient at nipping a careless finger both neatly and painfully. You normally did this only once. At each action a simple ratchet device in the machine rotated the ribbon bit by bit. From childhood I had peeped through booking-office windows at this magical machine and had heard its dull thump.

To reduce ticket fraud (the dodges they get up to!), the sequence of the figures making up the date was changed each year in a three-year cycle: 6JN27, JN6 28, 29JN6. It was convenient that each month could be decisively indicated by only two letters: JA, FE, MR, AP, MY, JN, JL, AU, SE, OC, NO, DE. During inspection, a keen-eyed ticket-collector would soon spot a fraudulent date on a passenger's ticket.

Another secret device to foil the fare-dodgers consisted of a wide range of design of the ticket-clippers used by station and train ticket-inspectors. Tiny shapes clipped into the edges of inspected tickets in code included triangle, square, half circle, diamond and others. Some clippers impressed code numbers in relief on the ticket, not easily noticed by the average passenger. Different numbers indicated to railway staff different stations or routes. This kind of information was contained in a private booklet kept at all stations. It was frequently crucial in tracking down those cocky people who preferred to travel at the railway company's expense and foolishly could not resist bragging about it to their friends.

Soon after I had finished my training in the booking-office, I was a little surprised to be placed in charge of the window one Easter Monday. Extra trains were run, and though our station was usually not over-busy with passengers, on this day great crowds queued at the window, taking themselves out for the day to various places of interest. When I came to cash up, I found I was a few pounds short. I felt really sick. The chief booking-clerk had been in the office with paperwork while I had been booking tickets, but there was room at the window for only one booking-clerk.

It began to come through to me that the shortage would have to be reported to the chief general superintendent at Derby headquarters. Certainly it would go against me. However, the clerks got together and made a collection on the understanding that I would make up the balance. This I could not do from my own resources, and on going home I broke the bad news to my father. Reluctantly he agreed to make up the amount, while I suffered agonies about the whole thing. I can't tell you how much I took my colleagues to my heart for their marvellous gesture.

Several months later in all innocence I fell into a cash trap that threatened my career when my honesty was questioned.

I was in the office alone one Wednesday morning. Snow lay thick upon the ground, and the wintry wind whistled furiously around the station buildings. Arthur Smallson walked in, as usual looking a little shabby in his uncared-for uniform suit. The only smart thing about him was his peaked cap inscribed in silver lettering 'Foreman', which he wore at a rakish angle. A good old stick, really. I was sitting cosily by the old iron stovepot and making a slice of toast for my breakfast.

'Morning, young Frank. I smelt burning so I called in to see if your office was afire. How are you?'

He didn't wait for an answer but gave me a couple of what I supposed were knowing winks which caused one end of his large black moustache to waggle.

'Frank, lad, can you lend me 5 bob on accounta me wages? I've seed stationmaster.' Another wink. 'Then you can take it outa me money come Friday payday. That's a good lad.'

As the station foreman in charge of platform porters, parcels porters and ticket-collectors on one of the two shifts, in my inexperienced eyes he was a personality of some authority. I went to the safe, took out 5 shillings from the float of £3 and handed it to him. In return, he handed me a piece of scruffy paper on which he had scribbled 'AS 5s/-'. I placed this in the safe as a receipt. I knew that, when we made up his weekly pay packet of £3 plus overtime in two days' time, I would be able to put the receipt note in his pay envelope, keep 5 shillings and return it to the float in the safe.

This routine went on intermittently for several months. On each occasion Arthur Smallson always included the words, 'I've seen stationmaster.' On reflection, I never recall him saying, 'I've had the stationmaster's permission.'

A porter on his shift, whom we called 'Ginger' Owen because of his shock of curly ginger hair and robust moustache, also on occasion borrowed 5 shillings on account of his wages. He too winked knowingly a couple of times and said, 'I've seed stationmaster.'

In my sweet innocence, I had not yet heard about some frightful and fearsome ogres referred to in station circles in bated breath – the district travelling auditors. The first eyeball-to-eyeball confrontation I experienced with one of these awful creatures was when I was alone and unprotected in my domain. The office door was suddenly flung wide open in the most imperious manner. In stalked a tall, well-groomed gentleman in a brown trilby hat, carrying an expensive brief-case, a lightweight mackintosh and a most charming smile. Two words would describe his entire demeanour: cheerfully brisk.

He glared at me over his horn-rimmed glasses of a style made popular by a young American film star named Harold Lloyd. 'Good morning, young man,' he greeted, briskly cheerful. 'My name is Mr Bennard, and I'm the District Travelling Auditor.'

You could tell his title was spelt with capital letters by the crisp way he pronounced the words.

'Morning, sir.'

'No trains due for a while, so I'll close your books.'

He removed his hat and mackintosh and hung them on the office door. Then he made a quick and professional dive straight for the safe. Naughtily, I had left it unlocked. We often did. He showed me no credentials, not even his travel ticket, which I presumed would be first class. Neither did it occur to me to challenge him. For all I knew, he could have been a suave gentleman burglar specializing in daylight robbery in railway ticket offices. But his brisk authority persuaded me that he was what he purported to be – a genuine District Travelling Auditor, DTA for short.

'My records,' he commented, 'show that you have a £3 float for change in your safe.'

'Yes, sir. That's right.'

He then turned upon me with the most charming and disarming smile you ever saw. But his voice was as hard as his clean-shaven face. 'Then why is there only £2.10s. here, and two tatty bits of paper which look suspiciously like IOUs?'

I had to stop myself from saying, 'They *look* like IOUs because they *are* IOUs!' But he had to be content with, 'I-I, er – lent the money to the station foreman and to a porter, sir.'

'You lent the money?'

'Yes, on account of their wages.'

'You lent the railway company's money? Good heavens, are you serious?' His smile had suddenly lost all its dazzle. His voice rasped harder. 'Does the stationmaster know about this?'

I became more miserable by the minute. 'I suppose so. Each time they borrow the money, they always tell me they've seen the stationmaster.'

His brows shot up. 'Always? Do you mean it's a regular arrangement?'

'Yes, sir. Most weeks.'

I began to think he was suspicious of me personally. Fiddling the books. What an awful thought. I could get the sack for this. I began to feel quite sick. Perhaps I was already looking guilty. My Dad will be really upset by this.

Mr Bennard went to the door. 'I'd better call the stationmaster.'

He returned with the relief stationmaster, Mr G.C. Gadd. Another booking-clerk arrived to take my place temporarily. The relief man took me into his private office and asked me to make a written statement. He had arrived only that week because our regular stationmaster, Mr Payne, was ill. I knew that Mr Payne would have trusted me implicitly.

The relief man spoke to me firmly but kindly. 'I don't think you have anything to worry about. But what you did was stupid.'

We were interrupted by a goods train steaming and rumbling through the station and rattling the windows of the office.

'I realize that now, Mr Gadd.'

'You'll also realize that I am obliged to make a report to Derby HQ. They'll expect me to make my recommendations. And I'll deal myself with the two men who talked you into this. I hope you've had your lesson.'

'I have indeed, sir. I'll never, never lend any of the railway company's money to anybody.'

'Good lad.'

I was glad in a way that I had had this lesson early in my career. At different stations over the years, I would be handling large sums of money to take to the bank and would draw large amounts to pay the wages.

Some three years later I was transferred to Derby headquarters, nearly forty miles from home, travelling there and back daily. A senior clerk on my section called me aside and told me, 'I remember that case of yours. Money being missing from the safe at Hanley.'

'Yes. Most upsetting.'

'Now that it's all over, I can tell you something.'

'Go on.'

'At one stage your job on the railway seemed finished. In fact, I had the task of drafting your letter of dismissal.'

I felt myself go hot at the unhappy memory. 'I was afraid myself at the time.'

'But we had a letter from the regular stationmaster after he'd returned from sick leave. He spoke very highly of you.'

'Thanks for telling me.'

Then he twitted me. 'Don't let it go to your head. You're at headquarters now. And you've got to carve a new niche for yourself. Good luck!'

In due course, I was to learn that travelling auditors swooped on all stations, large and small, in turn, twice a year. Nobody would know when they would arrive. To be otherwise, the objectives would be defeated.

Many years later one of them was to tell me a really sad story. A stationmaster at quite a sizable station had fiddled the books to the extent of several hundred pounds, which was equal to about six months of his salary.

'He pulled it off,' explained the auditor, 'by juggling with the amount carried forward as outstanding at the end of the month, and the relevant figure brought forward to the next month.'

'Yet it wasn't discovered?'

'Not immediately. He worked it out a month after my

previous visit, and I imagine he expected to clear it before my next visit. But he didn't.'

'What happened?'

His face clouded. 'I went round to his private office and asked him to come with me to the booking-office. He must have sensed that something was wrong. He said he'd join me in a couple of minutes, after he'd seen the train away. He was very cool indeed. Within a few minutes we could hear shouting and the blowing of a whistle. The stationmaster had jumped in front of the train.'

'Gosh, how terrible! Was he hurt very badly?'

'Very. The poor man had been killed instantly. And the station was disorientated. The place was in an uproar for an hour after that, believe me.'

Understandably, the travelling auditor did not disclose to me the stationmaster's name or his station, and I didn't ask him. But I knew that, before auditing in the Nottingham district where I met him, he had been based in Essex. In that county there are few stations of any real size.

Each morning the Hanley stationmaster, Mr Payne, carried the cash takings and cheques to the bank. He was usually joined by the stationmaster of Etruria, the next station down the line, on the same errand. Both wore navy-blue suits with brass buttons and black bowler hats. Most of the bosses wore bowlers. Judging by a whiff of our gaffer's breath on his return, there had been a surreptitious call for a convivial half hour. If any of us wanted a favour, such as a half day off for grandma's funeral, alias a football match with Port Vale or Stoke, that was the propitious moment.

In time I was deemed able to order money from the bank to pay the wages each Friday. Clerk Joe Sandham, a dozen years my senior, a cheerful chap over six feet tall with a mop of curly brown hair, kept an eye on me. From the wages sheets, it was my job to calculate the denominations of notes and coins – £1 and 10 shilling notes, half crowns (eight to a pound), 2 shilling pieces (florins), shillings (bobs), sixpences (tanners), those tiny, elusive threepenny bits (Joeys) and pennies (240 to the pound, coppers). I had to make sure I didn't finish up with only a mass of coppers or a batch of notes or whatever to fill the last few envelopes.

Amounts that went into the wage packets ranged broadly between £2 and £5 for a week's work including overtime and some Sunday duty. When Joe Sandham came to my table, I had just two more envelopes to fill.

He smiled. 'What's all this pile of tanners?'

He had spotted my dilemma. I couldn't possibly pay a man his week's wages in sixpenny pieces. His wife might hit him with the rolling-pin. By changing the sixpences with the ticket takings, we managed to make up those two pay-packets in appropriately mixed notes and coinage.

For a time I worked at Fenton station, a tiny station just over a mile from Stoke. A gentleman appeared at the booking-office window. 'Single to Kidderminster, please.'

I knew we hadn't a fare to Kidderminster. Only a few long-distance printed tickets were kept at Fenton. I looked in my record book for a fare but there wasn't one.

'I'll have to give you a ticket to Stoke, sir, and you'll have to rebook there for Kidderminster.'

The passenger bridled. 'That's rubbish, young man. This is a station. Kidderminster is a station. I just want a ticket from one to the other.'

Embarrassed, I could see the logic. 'Very sorry, sir. We haven't a through fare. There's so little demand. Tell you what. I could telegraph Derby headquarters and get a fare quoted within a few hours with luck.'

'Oh, Lord, this is ridiculous. I've got two heavy cases. I can't lug the things up and down the steps at Stoke just to rebook. It doesn't make sense.'

An idea struck me. 'I'll phone Stoke for their fare to Kidderminster, then add on threepence.'

This I did. It would save the man having to cross the lines. The passenger was delighted and tipped me a shilling.

The next time I was at Stoke station, I called in the booking-office and scrounged, unofficially, a copy of their fare list. After that, if a passenger wanted a ticket to a station not on my list at Fenton, I would look up the fare from Stoke and add threepence. Because I had in stock the tickets for local stations, the ones I made up with threepence were usually for long distances. Our stationmaster was based at Longton, a larger station, and his visits to Fenton were rather fleeting. I felt he had enough troubles without bothering him with a sub-station. I realized I wasn't working strictly according to the regulations, but it was a help to our passengers and increased the takings considerably at Fenton.

Some weeks passed, then a letter came from the chief accountant's office in London: 'Please explain your authority for issuing a ticket to Kidderminster when you have no fare on your books.'

I sent a reply, explaining what had transpired. Back came another missive: 'The standard instructions lay down the procedure for such cases. You should communicate with the fares office at Derby and obtain a properly calculated fare for your station. Please note for future.' On the railway, the chief accountant's department had a reputation for sticking rigidly to the official regulations, of course. If they didn't, the railway would soon be riddled with fiddles.

A few months passed and another memo arrived: 'It is observed that tickets to destinations for which you have no fare continue to be issued from your station. Kindly note that this practice must cease and I await your assurance that you will desist in future.'

Without consulting the stationmaster, which I realize in retrospect was a little naughty, I wrote again. I explained my actions, ending, 'It seems that the official instructions are creating inconvenience to our passengers. It appears practical for us to make up a fare by adding threepence to the fare from Stoke. If this contradicts the official instructions, would it not be more sensible to alter them?'

As with the other letters, I initialled on behalf of the stationmaster. Official instructions? They had been for-mulated at headquarters. Defiance could have been interpreted as Mutiny. Maybe ignorance will be my safest cover. Nothing more was heard from the accountants, and I continued my practice. Normally passenger takings at Fenton were small, but over the next six months they rose handsomely. On one of his fleeting visits, the stationmaster called. He showed me a letter, typed, from the divisional passenger superintendent's office at Derby: 'I am directed by the superintendent to congratulate you and your staff at Fenton for trebling your passenger takings during the past half year. Please provide a brief account stating how it was achieved, as it might form a guide for other stations.'

I felt myself go hot. The stationmaster asked gruffly, 'Well, me lad. How did this come about?' 'Me lad' explained.

'Hell, you've put me on the spot. Why didn't you ask me in the first place?'

'You're not here that often, sir. Besides, it didn't seem that important at the time.'

Suddenly the gaffer began to laugh. 'I've just had a funny thought. Because we are taking that much more money at Fenton, Stoke must be taking that much less!'

I just couldn't help laughing. 'That had occurred to me from the start. My aim was just to help the passengers, that's all. What's wrong with helping our customers?'

'I know all that, Frank, but what do we tell the superintendent?'

A terribly wicked thought entered my head. 'Why not the truth?'

'Yes, dammit. Why not! Seeing you are so good at writing fancy letters, draft one for me to sign.'

This was done. But the stationmaster was well aware he could be on the carpet for not asking the Derby superintendent before creating fares without the proper authority. And he couldn't very well blame it on his young booking-clerk!

Much to his relief, nothing was heard about it for some months. Then another letter arrived from the superintendent's department, signed by an assistant: 'The chief accountant informs me that you are issuing tickets to destinations for which you have no official fare. He states you have been creating through fares by adding threepence to the fares from Stoke, a practice that is irregular and must cease forthwith. Please acknowledge receipt.' To which the stationmaster replied as directed.

He was surprised when, some months later, he received another letter from the Derby passenger superintendent. It had a different reference number and was signed by another assistant, not the one who had formerly sent his congratulations: 'It is noticed from your half yearly figures that your takings have fallen to a third compared with the previous half year. I should be glad if you would be good enough to let me have your explanation.'

He showed me the letter. We looked at each other solemnly, then burst out laughing. We realized even more that railway accountants had a reputation for sticking rigidly to the official regulations.

There was a tap at the booking-office window. It was a young lady with a pushchair. 'Single to Lichfield, please.'

I was conscious of the stationmaster hovering. 'Sorry, madam, I can't book you to Lichfield direct,' I told her, more politely than usual. 'We have no through fare. I can book you to Stoke, and you'll have to rebook from there.'

'Oh, dear. That's a nuisance. I've got baby in his pushchair, and it's an awful drag to cross the lines at Stoke just to rebook. All those blessed stairs!'

'I know just what you mean, lady. Very sorry indeed. We don't get much call for tickets to Lichfield.'

'That's really silly. Couldn't you possibly phone Stoke and add a bit on from here?'

I gave her what I thought was a gentle smile. 'You might not believe this, madam, but it's more than my job's worth.'

4

The Men of Power Behind the Lines

Returning once more to Hanley station just after my
nineteenth birthday, I resumed my work in the booking-
office with greater confidence. I found myself enjoying it
more. It is surprising how much pleasure you get from doing
something you know you do well. All the chaps were willing
to help each other, and there was an agreeable family
atmosphere, a feature I was to find wherever I worked on the
railway. There were, of course, a few exceptions.

Mr Payne, a large and rather severe man, was a good boss.
One morning he called me into his private office. He had just
seen away the 10.50 a.m. loop-line train to Congleton. 'Sit
down, Frank.'

When the boss calls you into his private domain, you
worry. What have I done wrong? His gold braided uniform
cap rested on a chair in the corner, reminding me of his
authority.

He continued: 'I've got good news for you.'

All I could say was, 'Oh!'

'I've had a letter from Derby.' My heart missed a beat.
'They want you to work there. At HQ.'

My heart missed two beats. 'Oh gosh!'

His face broke into an amused smile. 'Do you want to
go?'

'It's a bit of a shock, Mr Payne. Yes, I suppose I do.'

He leaned back in his chair and lit his pipe. Soon he was
puffing out blue smoke and filling his office with the rich
odour of St Bruno tobacco.

'You start next Monday. How's that? They want you to
report to the staff office at nine o'clock. You'll be joining the
motive-power section to begin with, to see how you get on.'

'Yes, I understand, Mr Payne.'

'I expect they will give you a trial period.' He stood up and shook my hand warmly. 'I'm sorry you're leaving us, lad. Good luck.'

With all the excitement, I found myself breathing deeply. Butterflies disturbed the tranquillity of my stomach.

When colleagues heard, they said nice things. Joe Sandham smiled broadly. 'HQ, eh? Don't let it go to your head, boy. Anyway, all the best.' Such a friendly attitude I found humbling.

Derby! The very name sent a shiver of excitement up my youthful spine. In three years' experience on the railway, Derby, for me, had acquired an aura of mysterious power and authority, something akin to how good Catholics must feel about the Vatican.

Apart from the prospects of personal progress, Derby, I knew, would be a superb centre for seeing the crack trains that run to Leicester and London, to Sheffield, Leeds and Bradford, to Birmingham, Bristol, South Wales and the West Country, to Scotland, to Matlock and Manchester, to Stoke, Crewe, Liverpool, Chester and North Wales, to Nottingham, Newark and Lincoln. Many new places would beckon for exploration. At Derby I should be able to see some fine Midland Compound locomotives and Atlantics and Pacifics.

Starting on the Monday, I soon found travelling-companions, slightly older than me, who also worked at Derby HQ. Between Stoke and Derby, the journey of thirty-six miles took an hour. We amused ourselves in several ways. We played draughts and chess, read books and newspapers, did some study and argued fiercely and dogmatically, as only youth can, on the finer academic subtleties of political economy, religious beliefs, railway bosses and the goal-scoring techniques of our local football hero, Stanley Matthews: every one of us a budding iconoclast.

Two fellows, Tom Slaney and Les Warrillow, were choristers. The rest of us tested their endurance beyond despair as they tried to teach us madrigals in part-singing. We were even more out of tune singing 'Nellie Dean', 'Burlington Bertie', 'For Ever Blowing Bubbles' and 'Down at the Old Bull and Bush'. When the ticket-inspector examined our staff-tickets during a stop at Uttoxeter, he would joke with a phrase such as, 'Not much profit here. Your tunes won't earn much either!'

During the next few years I was fortunate in working in different sections at HQ – motive power, staff office, wages, coal distribution, signalling, operations, excursions, accidents, ticket frauds. Such a variety of work brought a broader understanding of the railway organization which should stand me in good stead if I stayed the course long enough.

I came to realize that there was a phalanx of clever people at HQ, a somewhat different breed from those I had known at local railway stations. They dressed more smartly, had greater self-confidence, dispensed authority with a natural ease and dignity – most of them, anyway! Yet I suspected that they, like me, had feet of clay hidden inside their highly polished black shoes.

In those first few weeks HQ staff seemed far removed from the realities of coal-fired steam-engines thundering round the country hauling passenger and goods trains. I soon learnt how wrong I was.

I came to know a good number of chaps in their twenties who showed real promise, and I don't mind confessing to a feeling of inferiority in those early stages. I knew instinctively that they had got something that I hadn't. But I was mad keen to learn. To catch up, I read avidly and attended night-school classes. After a while, I took lodgings in Derby near the Arboretum and built up a social life by joining clubs for dancing, roller skating, tennis and country walking, and I played my violin in an amateur orchestra. My friends unkindly described the sound I made as a 'vile din' but my conductor didn't grumble. However, I was no great shakes at sport, except shove ha'penny in the local railway social club.

Let me tell you about the power of men over men. Of the several departments at Derby headquarters – train operations, locomotives, carriages, wagons, permanent way, rules and regulations, accounts etc etc etc, the staff department, later called 'personnel', was the holy of holies. And that is where I was temporarily installed. If the high-ups had known that I was a secret budding writer, they would have said, 'Get the hell out of here!'

With seventy people in one of the main offices, it was a large set-up. Nobody smoked in working hours. Desperate chaps had to sneak off to the lavatory for a puff and a drag. You could see the smoke curling up above the cubicle and hear the rustling of a daily newspaper. I sat on a tall stool at a high, sloping desk and used a steel-nibbed pen which I dipped into a blue earthenware inkwell sunk into a round hole in the desk. Some superior people showed off their fountain pens. My duties consisted of filing, routine paperwork and running errands. Telephones rang, girl-operated mechanical comptometers clattered, conversation buzzed, clerks hustled around.

At the end where half a dozen young ladies worked the hand-operated comptometers, there were several vases of flowers. In all seasons you might buy sweets and bars of chocolates from a gentle, smiling fellow in his forties. His name was Billy Daywood. All you had to do was to leave the cash in the drawer and help yourself to the goodies whether Billy was at his desk or not. A colleague said his wife kept a shop.

Another budding entrepreneur named Jim Bowles, I was told, sold packets of twenty Players' cigarettes for 11d instead of one shilling, the standard shop price, so I approached him on tiptoes, so to speak. He glared, looked over one shoulder, then over the other and whispered fiercely, 'Who told you?'

'Oh, just one of the chaps.'

'For God's sake, lad. Keep it quiet. You could get me into serious lumber!'

Perhaps he saw his career being chopped in its prime and struggling with a mortgaged house full of wife and hungry kids, for Rule 1 in the Standard Rule Book of the LMS Railway stated unequivocally that 'Employees must not engage in trade.' However, his goods and my money changed hands in great secrecy. We might have been passing on military secrets to a foreign power. I smoked very little and couldn't see these high-risk secret deals that saved a penny a time on a packet changing my lifestyle very dramatically.

Basic work in the staff office consisted chiefly of matters to do with people, all most intriguing and fascinating. Hiring and firing, promoting staff and moving them from one place to another like a life-sized game of chess, arranging free travel, sick leave, retirements, discipline cases, trade union disputes, and generally managing the workforce. You can imagine that some cases were heart-rending.

For me at twenty, it seemed almost indecent to poke and pry into the most intimate and private affairs of a man's life, a few of whom I knew personally. I had access to many hundreds of personal files. Because they were highly confidential, a locked room at the end of our large office was their home.

Once, while in the files room, I came across my own personal file. Seeing my own name in large blue capitals on the folder gave me a funny sort of jolt. It could be shattering to see myself as others, especially the bosses, saw me. (Robert Burns put it much better.) I had stumbled on my file accidentally while searching for one on a signalman named Fergusson. Guiltily I looked around the room, peered through the shelves of files and saw another clerk there. I would wait until he left. But when he did so, another entered. I returned my dossier, frustrated. Then I wondered – is it a good idea to pry like this? It was not for my eyes but for others higher up. In four years on the railway, to my knowledge I had committed no great crime nor particularly distinguished myself. A boring file, to be sure.

I was puzzled at being able to see my own file. I learnt later that it was available because I was at HQ only temporarily during a trial period; if I stayed on, my file would be moved to a confidential set of files on all HQ staff.

I returned to my desk and handed the Fergusson file to my boss. When it came back to me, I scanned it curiously. Aged thirty-six. Married with four children. Fergusson had allowed two or three shunters from the nearby marshalling yard to enter his nice warm signal box for a brief break and a game of crib in the small hours when there were few trains about. They played for money, the naughty boys.

About two in the morning, Shunter Alex Burtt, a fiery redhead, had accused Ted Fergusson of cheating. A fierce punch-up followed. Ted was knocked over and caught his head on a steel signal lever. He was dazed and the chaps in a panic rushed to his aid. Bells of the telegraph instruments and the internal telephone were ignored. Consequently a freight train was held up at the junction several miles further back. This in turn delayed a sleeping-car express from Scotland. At the enquiry, all four men were disciplined by short suspensions from duty without pay, and an entry was made on their staff records.

Such a serious offence, which was not very common in signalboxes, resulted in a strongly worded circular letter being sent to all stations throughout the line. It stressed the content of Rule 72, which said, 'Signal-boxes must be kept strictly private, and signalmen must not allow any unauthorized person to enter.' A metal plate on signalbox doors warned, 'Strictly private.'

In the office file room the next day, my eye was again lured to my own file. As I held it, my hand trembled. Moral turpitude, or the fear of being caught? Who knows! I replaced the unopened folder. It just didn't seem right to pry.

I came across the file of Mr L.P. Briggs. This tall, frock-coated stationmaster of Stoke-on-Trent had, in 1927, interviewed me for a job on the railway and had personally recommended me for employment as a clerk. The sight of his paperwork gave me a warm glow towards him. According to his file, he was now at Nottingham, a much bigger station, with a salary of £550 a year. Mine was just £100. It would increase at £10 on each birthday until I was thirty, doubling my salary in ten years; £200 a year seemed like untold wealth.

Over the months I enjoyed wading through the personal files. A driver had allowed his unqualified fireman to drive his engine hauling a goods train; a booking-clerk had a bad record for timekeeping and was threatened with the sack unless he mended his ways; a goods invoice clerk had pestered the young lady clerk; a junior porter had climbed to the station roof for a lark; a young booking-clerk showing great promise in football was transferred, with his agreement, to another station so as to play for the divisional area team; a clerk had passed his internal examinations with distinction and had been appointed to a post as a stationmaster on a branch line; a shunter had crawled under stationary wagons in a marshalling yard endangering his life; a clerk had done well in the Institute of Transport examinations and was earmarked for promotion; a family man promoted to a post over a hundred miles away was helped with his furniture removal; following an illness, a steam-locomotive driver had been sent to a railway convalescent home in Dawlish in Devon for a fortnight; another had been removed from his job on the locomotive because of developing colour-blindness; a drama group leader sought approval to take his players to London in a railway amateur drama competition; a ticket-collector, having gained a qualification in first aid, was granted an extra day's leave with pay and an extra free travel ticket.

A station foreman who was a local councillor had been appointed mayor of his borough; a steam-locomotive driver drunk in charge of a goods train was temporarily reduced in rank to fireman; a railway police sergeant had been divorced; an alert signalman had prevented a serious accident; a family man in his forties was pensioned off because of illness; a goods porter had come up fantastically on Littlewoods Pools, and his resignation letter ended with a lewdness that would have made any respectable lady clerk who saw it blush to the marrow.

Any of these incidents, good or bad, that might affect a man's career prospects one way or another were entered on his personal record. Wherever he worked, these entries would remain until the man retired, resigned, was sacked, was imprisoned or took a fast train to float in that celestial warm-smelling locomotive steam that drifted into the heavens and wafted gently through the Pearly Gates. If a man's staff record showed he was accident-prone, he would be given another job to keep him out of harm's way;

otherwise he might find himself being wafted up there before his time.

In the room next to the files office, Big Bertha kept the stores and stationery for the staff office. Nobody called her Big Bertha to her face. She was large all over. Her iron-grey hair was swept up imperiously from her forehead. Tailored jacket and matching skirt in dark grey were her battledress. Miss Smith was a valued cog in the staff office machine in that she, personally, dispensed all items of stationery and stores as though they were her own property. On rare occasions, her normally severe face disintegrated into a dazzling smile that seemed to flood her storeroom with spring sunshine. Her desk, in the general office, was only a few yards from the storeroom door, which she kept firmly locked. She kept the key on a ring in her jacket pocket and never left them on her desk.

I called at her desk when my pencil was getting short. To my surprise, she said, 'Let me see your stub. That's no stub, young man. It's nearly half a pencil. Follow me.'

She led me into her guarded domain, switched the lights on – there were no windows – pulled out a drawer and gave me a small metal tube.

'Thank you, Miss Smith. What is it?'

'Haven't you seen one before? It's a pencil-economizer.'

I had heard recently that large organizations were noted for the massive waste in stores and stationery, and Miss Smith must have been saving her salary many times over. Even so, she was on the lowest scale. It seemed that on the railway ladies rarely got any promotion apart from typing-bureau supervisor.

The following day she was rushed off to hospital with appendix trouble. A young lady, a gentle soul in her early twenties, took her place temporarily and dispensed the stationery goodies with reckless prodigality. When Miss Smith returned to work after about eight weeks, she must have felt like Mother Hubbard whose cupboard was bare. There was quite a row about it, and the chief clerk had a circular sent round to say that each request would have to be made on a small order form and countersigned by a senior clerk. This system made Big Bertha even bigger in her new role. Yes, there was a rule for it. Rule 3 (iv) stated, 'Employees must not waste nor wantonly destroy stationery ...'

In the staff office, our seniors were always on the look-out for potential talent for promotion to stationmaster, station inspector, signalmen's inspector, traffic-controller, locomotive-inspector, locomotive shedmaster or supervisor of any kind. Much the same took place in the technical departments such as carriage-, wagon- and locomotive-building and repair, and in civil and electrical engineering.

If you wanted to get on in the railway, you had to be prepared to move about the country. Some chaps couldn't leave their home area, for various good reasons – children's schooling, sick or elderly parents. Perhaps a man was immersed in local politics or church work or engrossed in an absorbing local hobby or sport. He might even be genuinely nervous about working with strange people in a new area, as well as taking on a new job with more responsibility.

I found that generally if a young chap worked hard, kept good time, respected his superiors and was honest and conscientious, a good career awaited him. In our spare time we were encouraged to attend classes run by local officials, on managing a passenger station or a goods depot, and on the rules and regulations for railway operating. Lectures were free; so was travel to the lecture centres. Examinations were held and graded certificates issued to successful students. Details were entered on your staff record card.

Two other routes could lead to promotion. One was to be sired by a railway director with influence; perhaps you hadn't managed law, medicine, the City or the Church and fancied the railways. With many staff this system rankled, but in practice there were few such appointments. Anyway, they were usually civilized and charming chaps from public school or university who brought a little welcome style to the railway ambience. They generally received a good basic training in all departments.

The other route was through a privileged apprenticeship. Bright clerks were selected and given two years' training.

New entrants with high academic achievement came straight into railway employment and had three years' training. The system changed from time to time, and similar schemes were available on the other main-line companies. Trainees spent a few months in turn at a small station, at a large station, at a small goods depot, at a large one, in a marshalling yard, in an engine depot, in district, divisional and headquarters offices and in the technical departments. It produced good men, fit for a rewarding career. After the training, each man was expected to apply for vacancies in his range. After that he was thrust into the competition. Many excellent men have reached high office, some rising to general manager.

So that, my friend, is a peep into the working of the staff department at Derby on the LMS Railway.

I began to realize that people who had worked in the staff department knew an awful lot about everybody else, but everybody knew very little about staff people. It very quickly came through to me that staff people were very powerful fellows indeed. They obviously had the power of life and death over such minnows as I. Therefore, Ferneyhough, tread warily, breathe shallowly and salute frequently when within striking distance of a staff man, but never actually strike.

I noticed that most non-staff men were a little in awe of the staff office, slightly fearing those beings who were enormously, notoriously, terribly, frighteningly polite, especially when wielding one of their big sticks. And, Mr F., don't argue the toss with them. Always remember that your promotion, your prospects, your time off, your free tickets, your status, your pension, your very life is in their hands. They might even kill off your application to rent a patch of allotment on the railway embankment to grow your red cabbages and green peas.

Every few weeks a distinguished lady of style in dress and speech, aged about forty, came into our large staff office and sat at her desk. She became busy with her paperwork. Occasionally she would go into the chief's office for a session, then return to her desk for more writing. No doubt she had been discussing some important point of policy. Intrigued, I asked my colleague, Harold, who she was and what she did for a living.

He looked surprised. 'Don't you know? Why, that's Miss Wolstanbury.'

'I'm still no wiser, Harold. What does she do?'

'My dear chap, she's known far and wide as the Queen of Watering Places.'

'So what does she actually do, man?'

'Travels the country, visits the stations and looks after the interests of the lady passengers.'

He was leading me on. I must be dim-witted, for I was still puzzled. 'Come on, now. Give it to me straight.'

'Do you want it in officialese? She examines, reports on and makes recommendations for improvements to – wait for it – lavatories!'

'How disappointing. I thought she did something really important.'

'That *is* important. You ask the ladies!'

In our internal railway letters, those addressed to stationmasters began 'Mr'. Whether he was the stationmaster at London Euston or at Little Tiddlington-on-Sea mattered not a tittle. The time-honoured prefix 'Mr' was dispensed to all of them without fear or favour. But if you were a district officer, you were flattered with the accolade 'Esq.', being the shortened version of 'Esquire', which one discovered occasionally among the old and tattered correspondence of long ago in elegant copperplate script. 'Esq.' was doled out also to the professional hierarchy such as our engineers, solicitors, barristers and architects.

In headquarters, heads of small sections were 'Mr', heads of departments were 'Esq'. In the general offices, which were mainly of the non-smoking variety, some of those who carried 'Esq.' behind their names would walk with aplomb into any office with a full plume of smoke drifting by and curling about their heads, as from a steamed-up engine. They would also leave their hats on. The 'Mr' brand of fellow would never smoke in his office, nor in anyone else's office. And he would never, never walk into other people's offices wearing his hat. It did seem, some might say, on the face of it, that the confluence known as 'Mr' would have the edge on those known as 'Esq.' when it came to simple courtesy, but they would have to earn a few more promotions before they could afford the luxury of being recklessly discourteous.

Despite my years in HQ, I cannot recall ever seeing a general instruction explaining when to use 'Mr' and when 'Esq.'. You just waded through the various files to check on how things had been done before; then you could hope to keep out of trouble. Or you could ask your colleagues. Broadly, each had his proper level and place in the pecking order.

When I was first transferred from Hanley to Derby HQ, I was deputed to work for a decent and gentle senior clerk in his thirties, Mr Bernard Winson. With a natural courtesy, he always addressed me as Mr Ferneyhough. I had never been called that before and found it embarrassing, if flattering. Soon, among my regular colleagues, I was called by my first name. If, occasionally, someone called me by my surname alone, that was a language which screamed at me, 'I am important, young man, and don't you forget it!' To a man like that, I always said 'Sir'. You could tell he expected it. Besides, he might be your boss next week.

At the smaller stations, you weren't particularly supposed to 'Sir' the stationmaster, though very often the 'wages' or 'uniformed' staff did. To me, being young and ignorant enough to question the entire establishment, it was so much daftery, but I soon learnt that in a large system the operative word is 'survival'. And you just have to survive before beginning to thrive. As Bernard Winson, one of my superiors, had put it, 'You have to etch yourself into the pattern of the office routine.'

Times are changing. The standard Rule Book used to refer to employees as 'servants'. At some time before World War II, the word 'servants' was dropped and 'employees' substituted. Other documents were changed too. My copy of the Great Western Railway Rule Book had already made the change, but there could have been a Freudian slip printed on the first page: 'The following is a copy of the code of Rules for the guidance of all Officers and Servants of the Company, approved by the Board of Directors on 29th July 1932.' Signed – James Milne, General Manager, Great Western Railway, Paddington.

Times are indeed changing.

Gosh, that reminds me. I was appointed officially in 1927 as a railway servant, and I didn't bat an eyelid. I was just mighty glad to get a job on the railway, even as a servant.

5

The Pregnant Lady and the Mailbag Robbers

Masses of us at Derby HQ, clerks and administrators of all levels, found we were little more than puppets on a string. But who was working the controls? Mystery men in their ivory towers somewhere. In the late 1920s and early 1930s hundreds and hundreds of us were transferred by the trainload from Derby to London Euston. My move came in March 1934, when a nine-storey office block called Euston House had been specially built to receive many of us.

Derby had been the headquarters and centre of power for the Midland Railway Company ever since it had been formed in 1844. Euston had occupied a similar position for the London & North Western Railway Company since its formation in 1846. Throughout, they had remained deadly rivals, especially for passenger and freight business between the north and south. Then in 1923 they had both been absorbed, with thirty-three other companies, to form the London Midland & Scottish Railway. In the new group, the Midland and the Nor' West were by far the largest and the most powerful. They really threw their weight around.

Loyalties among railwaymen at stations and HQ for the old companies were powerfully fervent. The LMS man who was formerly Midland was the sworn enemy against anything tainted by the Nor' West. And vice versa. Though people didn't come to blows, fierce arguments laced with hyperbole were frequently exchanged, usually leavened with lashings of legpull and banter. Even the smaller companies such as the North Staffordshire and the Furness couldn't keep their loyalty from showing.

Snatches of chat in the office reached your ears. 'That's not the way we did it on the Midland.'

'I'm not surprised. Don't blame yourself. You were centuries behind the times, old boy!'

'Your old Crewe engines are always in trouble. They ought to be scrapped. Then we could have more of our Midland Compounds on the line.'

'Those darned things? The most unreliable ever built!'

But it was all taken in good fun. In the great tussle between Derby and Euston, each wanted desperately to be kingpin on the LMS. But slowly, inexorably, Euston finished on top.

That's why this little cog in that big machine had to seek lodgings in London. (Coming up to twenty-three and single, I would have moved to almost any corner of Britain as long as it was on a railway line.) I was soon settled in the signalling office on the sixth floor of Euston House. The new block had been opened a month earlier by Edward, Prince of Wales, who became King two years later but soon abdicated to marry an American divorcee, Mrs Simpson, with whom he had a passionate affair.

It so happened that the team of about a dozen I worked with in the new office had been my colleagues at Derby. They, in turn, had been drawn from the pre-1923 companies and couldn't resist having a go at each other in fun on occasion. They were still secretly proud of their old loyalties.

Now working in London, I was delighted at the prospect of traipsing round to see the main-line stations in my spare time. There I knew I would be able to view some of the finest steam-engines in the land and watch them steam away from the southern termini bound for the furthest fastnesses of the country. With free travel for holidays, I should be able in time to enjoy discovering some of the marvellous places that were the pride of Britain.

Knowing little about London, I had assumed there would be at least six or seven terminus stations serving all the lines into and out of the metropolis. Imagine my surprise when I discovered that there were, in fact, fifteen. Furthermore, all of them had been there since the turn of the century, some dating back to the 1830s. How could I have remained so ignorant for so long! Here they are in alphabetical order, with the railways in brackets: Blackfriars (SR), Broad Street (LMS), Cannon Street (SR), Charing Cross (SR), Euston

(LMS), Fenchurch Street (LMS), Holborn Viaduct (SR), King's Cross (LNER), Liverpool Street (LNER), London Bridge (SR), Marylebone (LNER), Paddington (GWR), St Pancras (LMS), Victoria (SR), Waterloo (SR). Totals by railway: SR 7, LMS 4, LNER 3, GWR 1.

I noticed a range of services offered to passengers, in addition to the usual refreshment rooms and telephone call-boxes, and a few shops and foreign-exchange banks. In the last century, it had been footwarmers. At 6d a time to hire, they took the pain and suffering out of any long journey during frost and snow. In more recent times, before the large-scale introduction of telephone boxes, you could send a telegram from the railway telegraph office. You could thus warn Aunt Agatha of your time of arrival at Taunton, Tunbridge Wells or Troon, or you could wire your business associate of your intended attendance at a meeting. From the catering department, a trolley would be trundled alongside your waiting train stacked with confectionery goodies, tea, coffee and soft drinks. Sometimes small food hampers were on offer, containing ham or roast chicken breast, salad, bread and butter, a piece of cake, a tomato and an apple. And a man in a white coat from Eldorado would be displaying a tempting choice of vanilla or choc-ice from a tray suspended by a strap over his shoulder or from a container on wheels. Newspapers and magazines could be selected from a slung tray by a boy wearing the uniform cap of W.H. Smith & Son or Menzies. If you were travelling with a friend or relative who was handicapped, a porter would bring a wheelchair to help you. This general air of service to the passenger amid the hustle and bustle of a busy station made me proud to be part of it. Ridiculous, isn't it! But it gets you eventually.

With Euston being at hand, I had the chance to see away many famous expresses. Not at that time having travelled all that far from home, it was those trains with the nameboards that really caught my imagination. My first sight of the words *Royal Scot* in tartan colours on a long board near roof-level at the side of every carriage on the train was memorable.

Some trains I could see in the daytime, others in the evenings. The names I knew by heart. The *Royal Scot* departed at 10.45 a.m. At 12.15 p.m. there was the *Mid-day Scot*, and at 1.20 p.m. the *Emerald Isle Express* bound for Holyhead to connect with a ship for Dublin. In the evenings a colleague, Reg Cook, joined me, and we saw such crack trains as the *Ulsterman* romping up to Heysham in Lancashire to catch a ship for Belfast. At 7.15 p.m. it was the *Royal Highlander* off to Inverness with a connection for the Kyle of Lochalsh, where a small boat would carry you over lively seas to the misty Isle of Skye. Then at 8.45 p.m. we could see away the *Royal Mail* to Holyhead linking with a ship for Dublin.

Back in the office I told some of my colleagues about a passenger who pulled the communication cord. While on a train from Euston to Crewe, my friend guard Gilbert Cosby explained how once he was in his van sorting parcels when he heard the vacuum brakes being applied. A look at his vacuum pressure dial showed the needle plunge well down from its normal pressure, which was nineteen inches to twenty-one. He could hear the steam-locomotive up in front still thrusting away. It then eased off a little. Gilbert was now sure that someone had pulled the communication cord and that the driver had noticed.

As soon as the train began to slow down, it whooshed into the short tunnel between Blisworth and Northampton. It so happens that the communication cord makes only a partial application of the brakes, and the engine kept driving hard against the partial braking so as to reach the platform at Northampton Castle station. Once there, Gilbert walked along the corridors to locate the trouble. Above the noise of the train, an agonized scream like a woman being strangled, suddenly smote his ears. In the corridor of the third carriage from the rear, he found a handful of people congregating.

He called, 'I say. Can I help you there?'

An agitated young man from the compartment called anxiously, 'It's my wife, guard. She's pregnant. And she thinks the baby's coming. We were going to her parents in Rugby.'

Another piercing scream came from the lady, apparently in labour. The husband's face was ashen. His wife was biting feverishly into his jacket, and she was being consoled by a middle-aged lady. Her face screwed up again in a convulsion of pain. Gilbert had told me he felt quite useless. 'Hang on, love,' he said. 'We'll be in Northampton in a minute, and we'll get you to a doctor.'

For something useful to do, Gilbert walked along the corridor calling for a doctor or a nurse, and a young girl responded.

'I'm a nurse. Can I help?'

'Yes. Follow me, please, Miss.'

As she reached the scared young wife, the train was approaching the station platform.

'Baby's not due for a fortnight,' confided the young father-to-be. 'I don't know what her Mum will say.'

By now the train had stopped, and the nurse said reassuringly, 'We'll get you up to the Barratt Maternity Ward. They'll look after you.'

On the platform the stationmaster was in attendance. When he heard about the problem, he called a porter quickly to fetch the wheelchair. The 'patient', looking a little more relaxed now, was helped into it, and husband and nurse wheeled her off.

'And that,' said Gilbert, 'was all I could do. I waved my flag, got the train away and sat in my seat in the van and completed my journal.'

All guards, of passenger trains or goods, carried a pad of journals, forms on which they recorded all relevant times and incidents for each journey. To account for this particular delay, Gilbert's entry read, 'Trn 9 mins late ex Npton. C/cord pulled. Preg woman put off for lcl hosptl. Clear run Rug.'

'About a month later,' he told me, 'I saw that young nurse again on my train. Said she worked at Northampton General. The baby was born that same night.'

It seems the young husband had been worried because his wife's mother wanted the baby to be born at her home in Rugby, but she was on holiday in Europe and couldn't be contacted. Not good timekeepers, babies.

When a passenger pulls the communication cord, it only partly applies the train's brakes. You can quite see that, if it put the brakes on fully, the train might be stopped in the middle of nowhere – in a tunnel, crossing a long viaduct or a few hundred yards before running into the next station. None of these places would be much use to a damsel being molested by an evil man, or a young woman whose pregnancy tries unexpectedly to come to a conclusion. The 'cord' was, in fact, a chain. But in polite society, it wouldn't be comely for an elegant lady to say it right out, bluntly, 'Guard, I just had to pull the chain.'

By the way, should any young blood think he can pull the communication cord just to show off to his pals, and get away with it, he would be in for an unpleasant surprise. Within minutes he would be confronted by the guard demanding his name and address. And in due course the joker would be fined a fiver plus the costs of the court. When the cord is pulled in the compartment, it hangs down a few inches in a loop. At the same time it turns a disc or peg at the top outside edge of the particular carriage. The guard, by looking out of the window of his door, can see which carriage by peering along his train. He can find the compartment by the hanging chain and can restore the chain to its normal tautness by turning the peg or disc outside.

When I worked in the accidents section at Derby HQ, I was continually surprised at the number of reports we received each week about the communication cord being pulled. All sorts of reasons were given – a nervous spinster lady frightened by a dog in the compartment, a man taken ill, men fighting, men drunk and disorderly, suitcases being stolen, girls being interfered with, a train failing to stop at a station as expected, an obstruction observed on the line, a 'funny noise' heard under the moving train, smoke rising from the side of the train from a hot axle box, lineside fire on the grass during very hot weather and caused by sparks from the steam-engine, and premature pregnancy threats galore.

A guard on the St Pancras-Manchester trains that stopped at Derby reported that a French lady, who couldn't speak English, had taken her small daughter to the toilet. By mistake, she had pulled the communication cord instead of the lavatory chain. And all she could say to the guard was, '*Oo là-là, Oo là-là! Je ne comprends pas!*' The guard had come in to the accidents office to explain to the chief clerk. 'Don't worry, guard,' he said. 'We'll excuse her the fine. And I'll write her a nice letter – in French.'

My friend Guard Gilbert Cosby told me of a nasty experience on the Scottish evening express from Euston. I was off to Glasgow for a few days and was in a third-class sleeping compartment on Gilbert's train. While the fun was going on, I was happily oblivious in dreamland. Gilbert had been along the corridor to give a passenger some train times. Returning to his van, he was shocked to see two men hastily opening mailbags. Certain that they had not seen him, he hurried back along the corridor of the speeding train to a compartment where, only minutes before, he had joked with a few soldiers. Tensely he explained to their sergeant, who was quick to understand.

Gilbert urged, 'Come on, lads, follow me!'

The sergeant and three men hurried along the corridor. In a body they dashed into the guard's van. The soldiers, who were marines and used to the rough stuff, took the thieves completely by surprise and quickly overpowered them.

Meanwhile, Gilbert, carrying out a procedure we on the railway know very well: he scribbled a note, weighted it with a pad of paper and placed it in an envelope. He leaned through the window and, as his train ran through Rugby station, threw the weighted envelope towards a porter standing on the platform.

With the two robbers safely under guard, in about three-quarters of an hour the train began to slow down as it approached Lichfield. This was thirty-four miles past Rugby. The train was not scheduled to stop at Lichfield, and Gilbert could assume that his note had worked. The railway police would have been alerted, and the signalman asked to place the signals to 'danger' to stop the train in the station, which would almost certainly have been deserted. Gilbert was banking on a police presence, and he was not disappointed.

As the train ran slowly into Lichfield station, one of the thieves made a dash for the offside door, jumped down to the

track and disappeared into the night. However, Gilbert's
envelope had worked wonders. He learnt later that the
runaway had careered straight into the strong arms of two
burly railway policemen. They knew a thing or two about
would-be mail-bag robbers jumping from a train on the
offside rather than to the station platform. The two thieves
were soon united once more – under lock and key.

When I left the train at St Enoch station in Glasgow,
Gilbert found me and started to tell his story. 'Come on. You
can fill me in with all the details in the refreshment room
over a cup of coffee!'

From guards' problems to ticket-inspectors'. One sup-
poses that Sunday work on the trains is hardly conducive to
a happy state of mind, except on payday. My friend
Kenneth Wheaton occasionally went home from
Teignmouth, where he worked in a bank, to Bournemouth.
His journeys posed serious problems for the railway,
because he went home on a Saturday, a journey of 110 miles,
and returned on the Sunday, 140 miles. The reason was the
absence of Sunday trains between Exeter and Templecombe.
The journey home was: Great Western to Exeter, Southern
to Templecombe, and Somerset & Dorset to Bournemouth
West. The journey back to Devon was via Salisbury and
Templecombe. It was most inconsiderate of Kenneth to
create an administrative enigma that was so bewildering.

One Sunday we travelled together. Half way from
Salisbury to Exeter in a full compartment, a travelling
ticket-inspector examined our tickets. Mine was a free one,
at which the inspector grunted. He was red-faced, in a
doubtful mood and elderly. He said to Kenneth, 'Five
shillings excess, if you please.'

Surprised, Ken asked, 'Why's that?'

'You're not on the direct route.'

Ken protested mildly. 'But I understand it's all right on
Sundays. There's no service via Templecombe.'

'Who told you that, sir?'

'Thought I'd seen it on a railway notice somewhere.'

'No. Definitely not.' He was getting testy now. 'Strewth,
the things what people says. I've heard 'em all. Come on

Llywelyn on the picturesque Vale of Rheidol Railway between
Aberystwyth and Devil's Bridge. It is the only remaining steam
train service owned and operated by British Railways.

The Gothic-style front of Bristol Temple Meads station, built in 1878. In the early 1830s Bristol merchants conceived the idea of a railroad linking Bristol with London and the Great Western Railway was born.

Weymouth between the wars, the only town in Britain where trains run through the streets, boat-trains bypassing the station to link with GWR ships for Jersey and Guernsey.

The author in his days as a stationmaster.

The manually-operated signalbox at Waterloo, London, Southern Railway, rebuilt by the London & South Western Railway in 1892.

Shunt-horse 'Charlie' at Newmarket station hauling the horse-box conveying 'Butch' on the day of his retirement. Horses continued working on the railway well into the 1960s.

This motorbus, fitted with wheels for either rails or roads, was a 1930 branch line experiment by the LMS Railway.

 100 YEARS OF PROGRESS
1835 — 1935

A poster celebrating the centenary of the Great Western Railway.

On the footplate of an 0-6-0 freight engine, a widely used work-horse that hauled passenger trains on subsidiary lines.

Fenny Stratford station on the Oxford – Cambridge line, one of 120 stations at which the author served during his years as a 'relief' man.

Frank Ferneyhough at home in St Albans.

Michael Satow's splendid reproduction *Rocket* running beside the Royal Albert Hall during celebrations for the 150th anniversary of the Liverpool & Manchester Railway in 1980.

George Stephenson, the 'Father of Railways', who started it all.

In the wet summer of 1973 this signalman had to wait some time before the stationmaster was rowed across the flood waters with sustenance!

now, sir. Five bob.'

Ken and I were conscious of listening ears and watching eyes. Ken said quietly, 'No need to be objectionable.'

Maybe 5 shillings were not worth a public showdown. Fellow passengers were careful not to become involved. Reluctantly Ken tendered two half-crowns. 'And I'll trouble you for a receipt, *if* you don't mind.'

'All them as pays excess fares gets a receipt. Including you, sir.'

This ridiculous altercation rather took the edge off what should have been an enjoyable journey. I had found the run from Bournemouth to Templecombe in that trundling old train on the sleepy and meandering Somerset & Dorset line quite enchanting. We chuffed away into delightfully romantic stations such as Stalbridge and Shillingstone, Blandford and Corfe Mullen in picturesque settings. It seemed that the tranquil surroundings had changed little during the past century.

I learnt soon after that weekend that Kenneth had confirmed at Teignmouth station that he was right. He also wrote to Southern Railway headquarters at Waterloo station in London. Their reply stated clearly that he could travel on the longer route on a Sunday without paying any excess charge.

A couple of months later Kenneth visited his home again. Hardly had the tall steeple of Salisbury Cathedral vanished from sight on a crowded train to Exeter than the same inspector appeared. His voice sounded disagreeable. 'All tickets, if you please!'

He seemed too engrossed in studying tickets to scan faces. To Ken he said, 'Five shillings excess to pay on this, sir.'

Ken said firmly, 'I don't think so.'

The other passengers sensed a row brewing.

'I'm telling you, sir. I want five bob. Come on. I've got a busy train to get through. Five bob.'

'Are you sure?'

'Sure I be sure. Five shillings.' He had his excess-fare book ready.

Except for the rumble of the train and the rhythm of wheels on rail joints, the compartment was tensely quiet.

'I think you're wrong. And I can prove it.'

He reached in his inside jacket pockets for his wallet and waded through old letters, holiday snaps, a letter from his friend Arthur about cycling in the West Country. But no railway letter.

'Oh, come on, sir!'

'I've got a letter from the railway somewhere. Just a minute.'

He reached his suitcase from the luggage rack, fumbled in his trousers for the tiny key. He felt all eyes were upon him. As he tugged at a spare jacket in the case, a pair of sparkling yellow underpants fell to the floor which a giggling girl, eyes averted, picked up. Something to tell her friends back home. Ken hastily screwed them into a ball and stuffed them back into the case. He found the letter and handed it to the inspector.

The official grumbled irritably, 'Nobody never told me about this.'

'That's no fault of mine.' Ken reached for the letter, but the inspector hung on to it.

'This ain't no legal document, sir.'

'How do you mean?'

'No date on it. So how do I know it's for 1935?'

Realizing he had lost the round, Kenneth paid up.

They could hear the inspector along the corridor, 'Tickets, if you *please*.'

Suddenly the entire compartment broke into laughter, and Ken had no option but to join in.

He wrote to Waterloo the following week, enclosing his excess fare receipt, and his original undated letter. Within a fortnight he received his letter back, dated, and a printed form together with a postal order for 4s 10½d. It was endorsed, 'Deducted for postage, 1½d.' It is not always easy for an ordinary passenger to comprehend the convoluted workings of the official railway administrative mind.

6

Secret Signs and Codes

Then quite suddenly marching orders. I was to be transferred from Euston to Bletchley, a small town in a bucolic setting in Buckinghamshire, with a population of ten thousand souls. Many were railwaymen, for it boasted a large railway centre on the main line, with branches to Oxford, Cambridge and elsewhere. My chief at Euston told me that this would present me with a real chance to see what the railway was all about.

After London, it seemed strange to be working in the comparative quiet of Bletchley, now my new base, but the eight platforms saw many trains in and out of the station day and night: local trains and long-distance express trains, including many with names, such as the *Royal Scot*. There were also local goods trains and great long goods trains, many of them loaded with coal from the north and empties returning for yet more coal.

I shared an office on Platform 8 with a senior clerk and a typist. Next door was the train and traffic-control office that was open day and night throughout the year. Five or six controllers were on each shift, and their work, mostly by telephone and large diagrams on the walls, mystified me and scared me a little. I didn't think I would be able to cope with such pressure.

My work was concerned mainly with administration and dealing with the problems of the large numbers of staff in various grades. Everybody seemed to work well together, and there was plenty of fun and laughter amid the various crises that frequently arose. The district control office had charge of about sixty stations on the main and branch lines. One of my jobs was to visit the Bletchley signalboxes to investigate the causes of main-line delays. An interesting feature I discovered was the make-up time that was allowed on many of the fast runners. For instance, the running time for a semi-express between Euston and Crewe might be, say, $3\frac{1}{2}$ hours. Extra minutes would be allowed in the timings for various sections, so if a train had been delayed for connections on the way at junctions such as Bletchley, Blisworth, Rugby, Nuneaton, Tamworth, Lichfield and Stafford, it could still arrive in Crewe punctually.

The parts of the route and the number of minutes (from and to) where make-up times were allowed were shown in the Working Timetables. As well as the train times shown in the public timetables, they included other intelligence – the starting and finishing places for the running of empty carriages and for engines running 'light' without a train; stopping places for engines, with or without a train, passenger or goods, to fill up their tanks with water; and other operating details. There was also a cunning little device in timetabling for which the timetable man who dreamed it up should have been awarded a TT medal. At large terminal stations and at junctions, you would find that the public timetable showed a few trains arriving, say, ten minutes later than the time printed in the Working Timetables. The reason was that the trains concerned tended to be late on occasion, so they always had ten minutes' make-up time. Delighted passengers would say, 'Isn't this train a marvellous timekeeper!' Passengers who did a lot of travelling often tried to get their hands on a copy of the Working Timetable, but they were issued to the staff very sparingly, and people used to write their names on them in ink and keep them locked in a private drawer.

For a few months in my teens, I had worked in the timetable office on Crewe station. They used massive diagrams marked at the top in minutes, and slanting lines drawn by hand running down the sheets. Where a fast train passed a slow train, one slanting line crossed over the other at the appropriate minute. Just to look at the things, never mind work out an altered train time, boggled the mind to the limits of disorientation. It was not really my scene.

My work at Bletchley also entailed collecting records of operations in the marshalling yards and some local travel. Gradually the real railway began to come alive for me. At

Bletchley, too, was a locomotive shed where I managed to spend time. I talked to lots of drivers and other engine-shed men, and the driving life came into focus.

Think of yourself like this. You are driving a train, at night, headed by a gigantic steam-locomotive. Just you and your fireman and all that enormous power. You are roaring through quiet countryside one minute and tearing through a town the next. And here and there a tunnel. You whoosh in, engine whistle screaming, throb through the Stygian blackness and whoosh out again, your ears going 'pop'.

Meanwhile your lithesome fireman is steadily stoking up that hungry, fiery-red furnace. The oil-lit headlamps carried on the front of your engine are not really for you to see where you are going. For the few yards of beam they are giving, you are virtually driving blind. Headlamps are for signalmen and other operating staff to know what sort of a train it is – express, stopping train, branch line train, fast freight, slow goods or whatever. This information is given by placing one or two lamps in different positions on the front of the engine.

Belting along at sixty miles an hour in the dark, the driver would see little other than those dots of guiding lights – the signals. He might also see the lights of a town or the moon when it is high. Signal lights, operated from the lineside signalboxes, show green for go, yellow for caution and red for stop. These are basics. There are other signals as well. Sometimes you saw a gantry with a confusion of signals on them. You could have all three colours showing at the same time, leading to different routes at a junction. Which one would be yours? Take a simple junction. If a driver approached a junction where one line veers to the right and the other curves to the left, at speed he cannot possibly make sure visibly whether the points are set for the route he is to take. But the particular route would be clear to him because one signal would be green and the other red. He would also know, because of an ingenious interlocking system between points and signals, that the points and the signal had been safely set for the one route.

You don't have to steer a steam-engine. That is why you never see a steering-wheel in the driver's cab. The driver must go where the rails take him. And the man who sets the points for the different routes is the signalman. There's a funny thought. It struck me before, not just like that. Signalmen steer the engine that pull the trains. By remote control.

Nor are there any gears. The driver works a handle called a regulator, to make the engine move. It works something like a car accelerator: you push it further to go faster. Another handle worked the vacuum brakes, to make it stop. My friend, if you happen to know a steam-engine driver, don't let him read this over-simplification; it's sure to make his hair to stand on end.

A driver is not allowed to work on any route until he has 'learnt the road' and signed for it on his route card. He would travel the route with an experienced driver who would point out the various features and idiosyncrasies – stations, signalboxes, junctions, level crossings, gradients, bridges, tunnels, marshalling yards, viaducts and various landmarks. He needs to be able to drive his train day or night, in raging storm, thunder and lightning, in dense fog or blinding falling snow.

Few steam-engines were fitted with speedometers. Most drivers scorned them. They reckoned they could judge the speed near enough. All a driver needed, to know the speed of his train was this: he should count the number of seconds it took to travel from one quarter-mile post to the next, divide into nine hundred, and the answer gives the miles per hour. And a driver didn't have to take an examination in simple arithmetic to qualify for the job. I don't think anyone told him how to see the mile posts in the dark. But you can't have everything, can you. Not for steam.

This dividing into nine hundred. You don't believe me? Right. Try this for size. Let us say it takes a train fifteen seconds to do a quarter mile; divide fifteen seconds into nine hundred, and you get sixty. So he is travelling at sixty miles an hour. If it takes the train fifteen seconds to travel a quarter mile, it must take one minute to travel one mile. One mile a minute equates sixty miles an hour. QED. This arithmetical calculation is official. It was set out clearly in the LMS internal reference book known as the Appendix to the

Working Timetables for all to see. And yet, in all my years on the line, I never recall its being referred to in working practice once.

Drivers weren't provided with watches, but guards were. The bulky pocket-watch was known proverbially as a 'turnip'; I know not why. Time-keeping is in the guard's hands. If a train were running late, he would be expected to save time at intermediate stations by speeding up the handling of parcels and mails and urging recalcitrant passengers to, 'Hurry along there, please!' In turn, the guard would expect the driver or fireman to be looking out of the engine cab, ready to accept smartly the guard's 'right away' signal – a wave of his green flag and a blast on his whistle.

If the train arrived at a station ahead of time, the guard would wait, standing with one foot on the platform and the other on the step of his van, turnip in one hand, green flag in the other, whistle in mouth, and give the signal to start – right on the dot. You can be sure that, if a train went a couple of minutes before time, you would get far louder screams from the passengers than you would for a train that was ten minutes late departing.

The road to becoming an engine driver was a practical one. A boy would start in the engine-sheds as an engine-cleaner. There's nothing like cleaning the muck and grime off an engine from top to bottom, and inside as well, to learn what made this great steam mountain of metal tick or, if you prefer, chuff. He probably wouldn't learn that George Stephenson, the father of railways, had originally put the chuff in the steam-engine, but he would soon come to know that the exhaust steam from the cylinders, in a steady rhythm, directed inside the boiler up the chimney, produced that beautiful sound that goes choo-choo-choo-choo choo-choo-choo-choo!

In the 1920s and 1930s the steam-engine driver was to schoolboys what the Concorde pilot was to become to boys in later years. Many a schoolboy nurtured dreams of becoming an engine-driver on the railways when, in their heyday, they were the fastest moving machines on earth. So the mates of our young engine-cleaner, coming home from work in the sheds covered in grime and grease, as evidence of working hard, would be full of envy.

Down at the sheds, one of the dirtiest jobs was that of cleaning out the smokebox. You came out looking like a coal-miner who had lost his soap and flannel. The engine would be standing on the rails over the pit so that the lads could get underneath. At the opposite end of the pit, another cleaner would be clearing out from the grate of the engine the hot clinker and hot ash. If the wind made a draught along the pit, the lad on the receiving end would be covered in white ash. He would look like a snowman. But the snowman could get his revenge. Seized by a call of nature, the cleaner at one end of the pit could direct his personal stream onto the hot clinker. It would produce a steaming stench that would ride on the breeze, grip the throat of the luckless cleaner at the far end and set him coughing, fit to fetch his lungs up. After that, there would be the usual vigorous exchange of impolite profanities.

At firelighting time on Sundays, when many engines were out of service, the shed was filled by foul and acrid yellow-brown smoke so tinged with sulphur that it fairly brought the tear ducts streaming away. A mixture of wood, wooden firelighters, small coal and rags soaked in oil was a common form to set an engine fire going. Depending on various conditions, it could take five to eight hours to breathe life and fire into it and kindle a roaring furnace, water boiling furiously, enough to send a jet of steam spurting and roaring through the safety valves. And all ready to go.

Simultaneously, the young cleaner would be learning about personal safety as he found his way around the engine sheds and the yard, busy with dead and live engines being shunted about. He would also learn that the tender of a really large main-line engine would carry five or six tons of coal on the top, and three to five thousand gallons of water underneath. High on the side of the engine, there would be the sandbox to fill. He would notice that the sand could be fed down thin metal pipes that led to the rails close to the driving wheels. Feed pipes were fitted both behind and in front of the driving wheels for journeys when the engine would run tender first, backwards. Sanding was essential when the driving wheels were slipping on wet or greasy rails, especially when starting with a very heavy train. Sand could be fed down the pipes either by falling through of its own weight – gravity feed, or forced through them by a jet of steam.

The young cleaner's first rides on an engine as a trainee fireman would almost certainly be in and around the engine sheds. Later he would try his shovel hand on a shunting engine in local sidings before moving up to goods trains and local branch-line passenger trains, according to his seniority in his depot enginemen's links. As the time went by and he continued to pass the examinations, usually verbal, he would qualify as a 'passed fireman': passed fit for driving. With years on the footplate, he would increase his driving skills. Following further instruction and examinations, he would become a driver in his own right, working either irregular or regular shifts, depending on the needs of the train services. As he moved up in seniority, one day he might rise to the main links, driving some of the crack steams of the day.

While at Bletchley, my next ambition was to become a stationmaster, so I spent some of my Sundays going out on the line with goods trains, on permanent-way repair trains and on engineers' trains working on bridge repairs, improvements to culverts and the like. For part of the way, driver Herbert Bayley allowed me to ride with him on the footplate in the cab of the engine, as we chugged along on the Bedford branch. Herbert, a typical engineman with a huge grey handlebar moustache, an inveterate pipe-smoker (usually thick twist), was in amiable mood and I wheedled him to let me put my hand on the regulator.

'Just for half a mile up to Ridgmont home signal, mind. Or you be a-getting me the sack!'

We had a dozen wagons behind our class 2F 0-6-0 goods engine, a remnant from the old Midland days. First of all, I gave it too much regulator, and the wheels spun round like mad without the engine moving an inch. The pistons were going in and out like the clappers, and the engine juddered so vigorously that I thought she would disintegrate into a heap of old iron. The young fireman laughed, and Herbert snatched the regulator back again. The engine subsided.

'Try again, lad, but go gentle, now.'

This time I was more successful and I got the train up to the fantastic speed of ten miles an hour. It must have been the juddering of the engine that made it seem fast. I could feel my face getting hot: from the furnace or excitement I am not sure. We had completed our half mile, Herbert applying the vacuum brake and shutting the regulator, in all of six or seven minutes, but it seemed an hour to me, I had lived so intensely during those moments on cloud nine.

We stopped for half an hour at Ridgmont for the permanent-way gang to unload their materials. We all three ate sandwiches, then chatted.

'Tell me, Herbert,' I began. 'What's so wonderful about a steam-engine, eh?'

'What d'ye mean?' He removed his curly pipe from his mouth, wiped his lips with the back of his hand and looked me straight in the eye. 'Well, mate, you can see it, you can 'ear it, you can smell it. And you can fair taste the bugger!' He laughed at this. 'Another thing. This one's got a sixth sense.'

'What, a steam-engine?'

'Yes. I'll bet thee that when we've finished us job at Bedford, I'll only have to whisper Bletchley in her ear, that's her home depot, you see. And she tears off like the bloody clappers! If that isn't no sixth sense, then I don't know what is!'

'Come on, Herbert, tell us more.'

'That's it.'

'You expect me to believe that, Herbert?'

'Yes, I'll tell you. She make a good stove for us cooking. I've only got to put a couple of rashers of bacon and two eggs on the shovel, shove the shovel in the firehole, and me breakfast's ready in two shakes of a shunter's pole. And you see that there gauge glass? You only 'as to fix an onion behind it, and you get the best baked onion this side of Euston!'

On the footplate it was scorching from the furnace and

dusty from the coal on the tender from a gentle breeze. Herbert started to talk about old railway photographs.

'Have you noticed,' he said, 'how all them railwaymen in olden times wore an 'at.'

'They still do, my friend.'

'And have you noticed how many 'as big bushy beards? We got a old picture at home of me old grandad. A Nor' West man, he was. He used to drive them Lady of the Lake engines with seven-foot driving wheels. Higher than your cottage ceiling. And his thick beard, it were ginger. Come half-way down his westcot.'

'Why the long beard?'

'On the old footplates of his day, they was open. No cab, you see. In the kitchen one day I asked him why he had a long beard. He said to keep his chest warm in winter on them open footplates.'

'Was he kidding you?'

'Don't know. I were only ten.'

When I first became immersed in steam-railway operations in Bletchley, I was intrigued by the sign and sound language of the natives. They put the Red Indians and their smoke signals in the shade. Day and night, railwaymen are passing signals to each other despite the rush and roar of the speeding trains and the shunting activities in the marshalling yards. Sometimes these are over quite long distances, alike in daylight or darkness, in thick fog or falling snow. Hands are waved, flags held aloft, handlamps are swung, detonators exploded. Hand whistles shrill, engine whistles screech, all to order. Many are in simple codes, and all are used in such a way that everybody down the line knows just what is intended and what is required.

So if a driver from Scotland arriving in the south received a hand signal from a guard who hailed from Devon, he would understand it. And though the LMS, the LNER, the GWR and the SR each had their own rule books, most of the rules applied to all the railway companies' lines.

Signals that most people know about are those given by the guard of a train to the driver, telling him it's time to start. He could tear up the platform to the front of the train and bawl to the driver, 'Right, Joe. Time to go!' Instead he stands by his van, blows his whistle and waves his green flag. After daylight he shows a green light from his handlamp. The driver acknowledges the guard's signal to start by giving a 'pop' on his engine whistle. As well as green, the guard is able to turn his lamp to show both red and white.

For any operations, if you can't put your hand on a flag, you may signal with your hands. There are five signals. Both arms held above the head denotes 'danger' or 'stop'. Either arm above the head says 'all right'. Either arm held out straight at the side, moving the hand up and down, means 'caution' or 'slow down'. Either arm moved in a circular manner away from the body means 'Move away from the hand signal.' Either arm moved across and towards the body at shoulder level says, 'Move towards hand signal.' At night a handlamp swung in various ways gave similar indications. Handlamps were lit by oil.

When starting his train, the guard gives only one short blast. One blast means 'go'. Three blasts mean 'stop', and two mean to run in reverse. These three codes are in wide use in marshalling yards and in the operation of goods trains.

You can't allow just anyone to blow a whistle and run around the place as though trying to referee a football match. Only a responsible person is allowed a whistle. What it conveys can be important and must be done properly and with great care.

What about steam-engine drivers' whistles which are worked by steam blowing through them? These are sounded on approaching tunnels, stations and level crossings. They are also used for approach to junctions. If a line divides three ways at a junction, a driver will give one whistle for number one, two for number two, and three for number three. This assures the signalman at the junction box as to which route his points and signals needed to be set. Usually the signalman knows ahead which route a train will travel. In the engine yards and sheds, various codes are used for the movements required – going to the turntable for the engine to be turned, to the water-crane road to take water, to the coal-loading line or out onto the main line itself.

Cause of much amusement to strangers was the crow. It was done in a rhythm similar to that of the crow of the farmyard cock to proclaim proudly that he is studmaster to his entire harem, cock-a-doodle-oo. This code was applied when a train was being 'banked' at the rear, when, for instance, assisting a goods train up a steep incline. From a stand, the driver of the front engine would give two crows, and two crows repeated by the rear engine would be his acknowledgement. Strangers passing by have been known to think that the drivers exchanging 'crow' whistle codes were just having fun, possibly trying to make the cocks at any nearby farm jealous.

You won't be surprised to know that enginemen among themselves had a whole collection of private whistle codes – the tea's made, there's a boss around, see you in the canteen, book off duty, I've left a note in your locker, we will want coal and water, it is a dirty fire, mate!

One young driver, newly married, often whistled a message to his adored wife as he drove his goods train past Ridgmont, where they lived. He sent long-short-long, which, in the code devised in the last century by the American Samuel Morse, meant 'k'. And between the young lovers, it stood, of course, for 'kisses'.

In the winter months especially, with murky fog around or falling snow, we heard the detonators explode as wheels ran over them on the rails. In such poor visibility, fog signalmen were positioned near the signals, and detonators were placed on the line when the signal was at danger or caution. (They were clipped on the rails by the lead strips attached to them.) Detonators were additional to the signals the fog signalman gave by flag or handlamp. He would show green for 'go', red for 'stop' and yellow for 'caution'. Men for fog signalling duties were normally drawn from the permanent-way gangs. What a boring and tedious job it could sometimes be! At some places, a small hut and a fire brazier were provided, to give the poor chap a modicum of comfort.

Detonators were also used to give protection to gangs of men working on the line. Another use was on those occasions when a train was stopped somewhere on the line without the protection of the signals. Three detonators would be placed on the rails ten yards apart, three-quarters of a mile in rear of the train, plus one at a quarter and one at half a mile behind the train. When a fast train came along, the explosion of the three detonators would go off bang almost at the same time and be louder than just one.

Bletchley was a super place for seeing some cracking good trains tearing through on its up and down fast lines. Hardly an hour passed without a real beauty displaying power and speed. Those going north travelled to Scotland, Liverpool and Manchester, Birmingham and the Lake District.

Behind the scenes, there was always much argument about the value of the really fast expresses, and the argument raged from top to bottom in the railway passenger business. Certainly much public interest had been stimulated by those trains endowed with their own attractive names, from the *Cheltenham Flyer* to the *Atlantic Coast Express* (*ACE*), and from the *Highlandman* to the *Sunny South Express*. In the 1920s and 1930s these were just four out of nearly a hundred. All had their own special entries in the separate timetables of the four main-line railway companies, and competition was strong among them. Named trains enhanced the publicity value to the railways. Passengers clamoured for seats on them. There was far more prestige and style in travelling on the *Royal Scot* than in riding on the mundane 10.45 a.m. from Euston to Glasgow.

Apart from the competition between the different railway companies, there was the growing competitive bite from the motor car and the motor coach. These vehicles offered a door-to-door service, and the costs were lower. In the 1930s the influence was so great that the railway companies had to go to the government, cap in hand, for financial help towards modernizing their signalling and trains.

Operation of the glamour trains brought their own problems. They needed much more space ahead – headway, as they gobbled up the track at breakneck speeds. Many slower trains, both passenger and goods, had to skedaddle smartly out of their way. This I knew intimately from my operating experience.

For signalling purposes, the lines were divided into sections, the signalboxes marking the dividing points. Sections could be any distance from a quarter of a mile to several miles. Normally only one section of the track was needed to separate one train from another. But the very fast trains, competing for space against the stopping trains and the slow local goods trains, needed two or even three sections ahead to be kept clear of other trains.

You can quite see where the costs mounted. When a fast express was delayed, it held up other trains in its wake. Long delays were often inflicted on lengthy goods trains. Most goods wagons were not fitted with automatic braking; they had only hand brakes. With the wagons being loose coupled, metal buffers clanging, goods trains took longer to start and get up some speed, and longer to stop. Long goods trains were indeed slow runners and for many miles would average only between thirty and fifty miles an hour. To get them out of the way of an oncoming express, they often needed to be shunted, in good time, into a siding or from one running line to another.

In my frequent rides with the goods guards in their goods brake vans, I never found much comfort, just adventure. With loose-coupled wagons, the couplings hung down loosely when the buffers were touching each other. When the buffers were well apart, the couplings were taut. You can see what's going to happen, can't you? If they are loose when the engine begins to pull, that on the first wagon will become taut, and the next and the next, and the next with decreasing intervals. The goods brake van is stationary until your coupling is suddenly pulled taut, and then you could be jerked severely.

When the goods train begins to slow down to stop, the reverse happens. As soon as the engine stops pulling, the couplings lose their tautness, starting with that nearest the engine. From the van, you can hear the wagons clanging together at a rapidly increasing pace, and the vehicle to suffer the greatest bump would be the brake van. When I have been in the goods van in these circumstances, I have watched the goods guard grip the handrails tightly to brace himself in a panic for that final bone-shattering impact, and I have done the same. Sometimes a guard has been off his guard, so to speak, and has been injured by being flung across the floor of the van.

So you can see that, with crack expresses sharing the lines with the slow movers, the expresses were a costly business. But obviously the railway managements considered they were worth it, for the consequent image-building and prestige. I am sure they were right. Perhaps one day goods speeds would more nearly match passenger trains.

In the way that passenger trains suffered by competition from the car and coach, so goods traffic of all kinds lost tremendous business as the motor lorry progressed. But that's another story.

At Bletchley station, today, Tuesday, had been chosen to be Annual Fire Drill Day. It was often an excuse for youthful horseplay. About a dozen of our staff – porters, a ticket-collector, a signalman, guards, shunters *et al.* were volunteers to take part in the drill. I was the only clerk in the team.

A lull between the trains in mid-morning had been selected, and the drill was expected to take less than an hour. In charge was a head shunter named Terry Clarke, acting as captain. He delegated men to inspect all the fire buckets on each of the eight platforms. Bright in post office red, they had the word 'FIRE' painted on them in black. One bucket standing on a bench on Platform 1 was filled with soil and was growing a dozen brilliant yellow daffodils. They were in front of the general office, and from the inside the chief clerk and his young lady assistant could see them nicely, thank you.

Captain Terry shouted, 'Eh, George, tip that lot on the rubbish heap and fill it with nice clean water what's proper with a fire bucket!'

There was little reaction from the senior clerk except to come out of his office in his bowler hat and wail plaintively,

'You might have saved the flowers!'

We temporary firemen, enthusiastic in an extra-curricular function and enjoying the break from routine, would earn 5 shillings each, due on the next payday.

Another fire bucket was discovered on Platform 3, also behaving 'out of character'. In fact, it was behaving disgustingly, as a receptacle for an empty Woodbine cigarette packet, a half-eaten sandwich, stale orange peel, a couple of apple cores, sundry cigarette ends, used matches, an empty sardine tin, three empty beer bottles, an empty embrocation bottled labelled 'Sloane's Liniment' and other random rubbish.

Our next job was to check the location of the water supplies, make sure there was a strong flow of water and see that all fire hoses were rolled up correctly and in their appointed locations.

After that, we went to the sidings, where a large metal rig, wrapped in oily rags, had been set up as a facsimile fire hazard. The idea was to light it, then, on the word 'go' from the captain, for a small team to rush to a fire hose, connect it to a water supply, unroll the hose and turn on the water supply, run up to the fire hazard and play the jet of water on it until it was completely extinguished. The stationmaster attended for this final item. He took the demonstration quite seriously compared with our occasional fooling around. We had so few fires on the railway – on trains or stations or elsewhere – that we regarded it as a great joke. Still, the captain made us do a good job of things. He timed us. 'Just three minutes. Half a minute faster than last year. Good work, lads.'

The stationmaster commented, 'Well done, chaps. We know we've got a good firefighting team together. Now back to your jobs.' He grinned amiably and walked back to the station.

Young Bertie Watts, a shunter, was emptying a hose on the station platform. Bertie would do anything for a laugh. He lifted the hose, pointed the jet to the slightly open window of the senior clerk's office and let the last flush of water spurt through. Out rushed the senior clerk, angry now. He shouted, 'You've destroyed my daffs and now you're trying to drown *me*! What next?'

Returning to the sidings to tidy up, Bertie took hold of another hose lying on the ground and still connected to a water supply. He splashed his jet onto a shunting engine, creating a fiercely hissing cloud of steam. Down jumped the burly fireman from the footplate, caught hold of Bertie, grabbed the hose and gave the lad a thorough dousing. He took it in a sporting way.

Both the fireman and his driver enjoyed this piece of harmless nonsense. But the captain bawled, 'Eh up, Bertie. Fire drill's a serious business. Any more of this and I'll have your five bob stopped!'

With the captain, I sauntered across the station overbridge to our depot office on Platform 8. He made an entry in the logbook among notable items of the day. This was scrutinized daily by the district controller himself: 'Fire drill carried out as per Regulations between 10.25 a.m. and 11.10 a.m. Checked all Fire Buckets, Hoses, Water Supplies, and put out Fire Hazard in Three Minutes. Half a minute faster than last year. All Correct Without any incidents – signed, Terry Clarke, Shunter, (Act'g Capt.).

7
Scared by a Fierce Bull Mastiff

While I was getting on with my paperwork that sunny morning in April, in the depot office on Platform 8, the senior clerk walked in. 'The boss wants to see you.'

The typist teased, 'You're getting the sack. I forgot to tell you!'

Off I went along the platform and knocked on the district controller's private office door.

'Congratulations, Ferneyhough. You start next Monday as a relief stationmaster.'

It really took me back for a moment. 'Thank you very much, sir. Where will I be based?'

'Here at Bletchley.'

He was a nice old gentleman, all of fifty-eight. He's not nice just because he's giving me a new job. He was always nice. Mr Hampson had a car and played golf and came to work at half past nine and went home at half past four on most days, except when emergencies arose. Only a gentleman could get away with that.

'Bletchley! That's just marvellous.'

'It's a disappointment for me, my lad,' he joked. 'I thought we were going to get rid of you. I was hoping it would be Carlisle or Swansea or Holyhead!'

A week earlier I had been to Derby for grilling in the rules and regulations by a tough head-office inspector. The railway doctor ran his stethoscope over me and pronounced that I would live. My eyesight was also tested.

Having been working prodigiously at Bletchley for a few years, I knew I would have plenty of friends about the area and generous help when needed. I would also be able to keep my excellent lodgings with the young Lucy and Bert Cobb. During those years I had attended classes in the operating rules and regulations, in passenger station and goods depot working. Of my various internal certificates, I had been

lucky enough to get one first with distinction and another
first-class pass.

Stationmasters and clerks were entitled to two weeks
holiday. They ranged from early in April to late in October.
My summer consisted of two weeks here and two weeks
there. My territory lay on the main line between Tring and
just south of Rugby and included all the branch lines. In the
winter months I took relief clerk jobs, assisted with special
work when and where needed and occasionally checked the
outstanding accounts. What better training for promotion to
better things? And, of course, not a chance of becoming
bored.

Usually in February, the holiday dates were circulated
among the staff. You didn't have any choice. Headquarters
at Derby supplied you with your dates and that was that. It
was no good saying you wanted to go a month later to take
your mother-in-law or enjoy a spell at the races. And if the
dates mucked up your kids' education or messed up your
family life, it was just too bad. It was the rule, and you
accepted it. But if there was anything really dire, HQ would
normally see what could be done for you.

If I were in charge of a station for a week or more, I had to
test the books for any money not paid, investigating
accounts for four different firms or individuals. You can
imagine the embarrassment. I would arrive at a firm's office
and ask for someone in authority. 'I'm deputizing for Mr
Smith, the stationmaster on holiday. I see you owe the
railway £45. Is that in order, sir?'

This was work I didn't like a little bit. At Leighton
Buzzard one firm's manager, Mr Grimley, a short, thick-set
balding fellow in his forties with a voice like a foghorn,
became almost violent. Even his secretary blanched.

'Come into my office, Mr Whatsername. You say £45 is
still owing on your books?'

'Yes, that's right, sir.'

He thumped the heavy oak desk. 'And do you know why
it's still owing? Don't interrupt me! I'll tell you why. I said
don't interrupt! It's because we haven't bloody well paid it.'
He paused to get his breath. 'And do you know why we

haven't paid it? Shut up! It's because it isn't due till Monday week. For God's sake, sit down, man. Instead of bouncing from one foot to another!'

'I beg your pardon, sir. But I really do know all that.'

With some asperity he demanded, 'Why all the fuss, then?'

'No fuss at all. You've confirmed that you haven't paid the bill and that it is still outstanding on my books. That's all I needed to know. Many thanks, sir. I'll bid you good-day.'

'No, you won't, young fellow. Tell me this. Does Mr Smith know you're doing this behind his back? You are doubting his honesty. He's been an old friend for years, and I resent it.'

How could I get out of this impasse!

'Mr Grimley, you'll know that, in business, spot checks have to be made of the credits. This is to protect our railway customers, people just like yourself. Suppose you had paid it and a dishonest stationmaster had pocketed it!'

That stopped him in his tracks. He stroked his chin and looked thoughtful. 'By gad, yes. I believe you've got something there.'

'Not really me, sir. I'm merely carrying out official instructions.'

'Is that so? Then you're nothing but a bloody post office!'

He was becoming more relaxed and I added quietly, 'You'll agree this should be confidential. Between you and me. Right?'

'Right. And right. Get back to your station and play with your little trains. And I'll send you a cheque a week on Monday.'

He grinned broadly as he showed me out of his office.

A much more tricky case faced me at Islip on the Oxford line. Colonel Adrian Pikesby, retired from the Royal Engineers after World War I, was building up his small business as a specialist dog-breeder. He was every inch the retired military officer: tall and soldierly, trim moustache, hair grey and thinning. He usually wore a sports jacket, whipcord breeches and brown leather leggings, a style of dress popular in farming and hunting country.

I worked at Islip for some weeks while the regular stationmaster was on sick leave in the summer. I had looked up trains for the Colonel and had handled, in the goods yard, some of the equipment he needed for his establishment. Though there was a gap between our ages and social status, we enjoyed a pleasant rapport.

The small station was quiet, and we sat together on a platform seat enjoying the sunshine as he smoked his pipe.

'Colonel, may I speak confidentially?'

'Of course, dear chap. Fire away.'

'I believe you know Farmer Gregston up at the Red House Farm?'

'Who doesn't! He's the most awkward bugger in the county. Should have been shot years ago. We're sworn enemies on the Rural Council, and I, er, well ... what's your problem?'

'He owes us an account of about £32, and he's sent a note through the post that there's a cheque waiting, if I'll call and collect it.'

'So?'

'He's got that bull mastiff on a long lead. It's just by the entrance and I can't get near the place. I've tried three times already, and my HQ are pressing for settlement. Any ideas?'

He tapped the ash out of his pipe, then began to refill from a brown pouch in crocodile skin.

'M-m. Ah!' Then his leathery face suddenly crinkled into a wicked grin.

'Colonel, the suspense is killing me. What is it? It's got to be good.'

He simply roared with laughter, intriguing me even more. 'My dear chap,' he grinned. 'It's the easiest thing in the world. When you know how. I'll tell you how to beat old Gregston. Give him a ring and tell him you'll be up at his place in the morning for the cheque.'

'But how do I get past that dog?'

'Look, I'll pick you up tomorrow in the jolly old jalopy, take you to my place, then drop you off near the old bastard's farm. And I'll wait for you while you get the cheque.'

'What then, Colonel?'

'You just walk up to the farm, pat the dog gently, then go to the house to get the cheque.'

'I'll do as you say. Won't you tell me more?'

'Ah, all will be revealed tomorrow, chappie. My system has never failed. See you in the morning.' And he left the station whistling, appropriately, 'Daddy wouldn't buy me a bow-wow.'

At nine o'clock the next morning I walked into the booking-office and said to Bill Blakesby, the booking-clerk, 'I'm off to Farmer Gregston's place to collect that account. It's ages overdue. I'll be back in an hour.'

Bill chortled and placed a sixpence on the table. 'Cover that. I'll bet you a tanner you can't get past their dog.'

'I don't bet on certs, Bill. But you can buy me a pint if I get it, and I'll buy you one if I don't.'

'Good. You've lost before you've started!'

Within minutes I heard Colonel Adrian Pikesby's nifty 'jalopy', a red Triumph Gloria sports type, roaring outside, and soon we were away. Within the hour he had dropped me back at the station. I marched straight into the booking-office, cocky as hell. 'Put that with the cash to bank, Bill.' This brought me a *frisson* of pleasure.

I began to walk out with not another word, just to provoke him. He called me back and looked at me with flattering admiration.

'Mr Ferney, you're a genius. No stranger has ever got past that bull mastiff. You must have guts, mate.'

I spoke casually. 'It was no trouble, Bill. When you're a relief stationmaster, you have to cope with all sorts. Trains derailed, death and disaster in the tunnels, thunder and lightning in the marshalling yards ...'

'Oh, come off it.' He kept on chuckling to himself. 'I just can't believe it. Won't you blow the gaff? If you don't, I won't sleep tonight!'

'Right. First, you owe me a pint. Second, Colonel Pikesby lent a hand. Almost literally, lent me a hand.'

When I explained to him what we had done, he laughed and laughed and laughed. Tears ran down his chubby cheeks. When he had recovered, he conceded. 'You deserve that pint!'

When the Colonel had picked me up earlier that morning, he first drove me to his establishment, a small farmhouse with outhouses of timber for the dogs. He explained that he had a bull mastiff bitch on heat. She was a large dog, big enough to take a pony saddle and stirrups. He asked me to stroke her and to fondle her intimately, then we drove off very fast to Gregston's place. The Colonel dropped me near to, but out of sight of, the farm, and off I went on foot.

When I was within several yards of the dog, the large animal bared his teeth and barked and bounced about. He looked so fierce that he fairly scared the daylights out of me. Was I making a stupid mistake? A warm and gentle breeze was drifting my way, and I moved down wind. The animal stopped his barking, then began to look around, sniffing the air. Nearer and nearer I stole towards him, my heart pumping violently. Now really close, I saw him looking at me. He even wagged his tail. With little experience of dogs, I was finding this fascinating.

I called him gently by name, Caesar, and he began to make crying and whimpering noises. I reached out to stroke him and he fussed me up, licking my hand hungrily as I sidled past him and strode up to the farmhouse door. Oh, the relief of it! I pulled a handle which clanged a noisy bell deep in the recesses of the house. Soon a maid appeared.

'Mornin', sir. Be you the stationmaster? Mr Gregston, he says to give you this.'

I thanked her for the envelope, which I pocketed, and made my way back towards Caesar. He was still friendly and expectant but not so excited. Bravely I took a chance and stroked him, then walked as fast as was decent to the Colonel's car. Before reaching him, I opened the envelope to make sure the cheque was there. Yes, the figures of £32.14s.6d. were clear to see, and a note which just said, 'Mr Stationmaster, Congratulations.' My worry receded.

I fairly bounced into the Colonel's waiting car and, as he drove me back to the station, I told him the good news and thanked him profusely. 'My pleasure, dear boy. Just an old dog-breeder's trick, that's all.'

In the early afternoon, Bill put the cash for banking in a leather cash bag, sealed it with red sealing wax, handed it to the guard of the afternoon train to Oxford and got him to sign for it in our cashbook. There was no bank in Islip village.

The next morning I received a telegram over the railway telegraph network instructing me to take duty from the following day at Althorpe Park and saying I would be replaced by another relief man.

Bill said, 'It's always the same. As soon as you get used to one reliefman, off he goes and you have another.' He was opening the few letters that had arrived by the morning's post. Suddenly, he shouted, 'Oh, no!' Laughing aloud, he passed me Gregston's cheque with a note from the bank. 'I can't believe it,' he snorted. 'The damn thing's bounced!'

'Bounced?' I felt absolutely livid. 'What the hell! Figures agree with the words. Date's all right, 20 June.'

Bill scrutinized it. 'Oh, look, the cunning blighter. He's made it out for June next year!'

Well, what could you do but laugh.

'That's a job for the new man who arrives tomorrow. I shall have new problems at Althorpe Park!'

'Right, Mr Ferney. But don't forget, you owe me a pint.'

Occasionally I worked at Bicester. As well as the station on the Oxford line, I was responsible for the Great Western station across the town. There, in the afternoon, I received a call on the post office telephone.

'Hallo!' panted a lady, sounding very distressed. 'Is that the stationmaster? Oh, good. There's a railway carriage running away. By itself. Just saw it from my car. I'm in a call-box.'

I paused a moment, then it struck me. 'Oh, that's all right, madam. It's quite safe, I assure you.' I gave her time to get her breath back. 'It's what we call a slip-coach.'

'A what?'

'Slip-coach, madam.'

'Oh, thank goodness. I thought it was heading for a

terrible crash. But what is a slip-coach, pray?'

'It's a carriage which is automatically slipped off the back of an express.'

'Strange, but I've never heard of it before. I always go by car. What's it for, anyway?'

'A second guard in the last carriage disconnects it from the express. While it's still running, you know. So the express keeps up its speed and doesn't have to stop.'

'I see.'

'In fact, the carriage is already here in the platform. Safe and sound, madam.'

'That's really clever. Thank you for telling me.'

In turn, I thanked the lady for her call. It seems that she was a stranger in these parts, for the slip-coach had been a familiar sight on this route for many years. The system allowed passengers to enjoy an express service from Paddington to Bicester without the express train itself being stopped and delayed.

Quite a lot of passengers over the years have refused to travel in a slip-coach. Maybe they thought the guard would doze off and forget to work his connections, or slip them off at Banbury instead of Bicester, or even take them on to Wolverhampton. I can't see what they were worrying about. They could always pull the communication cord!

Surprising to many people, a system of slip-coaches had been used on the London and Blackwall Railway since its opening in 1840. For some years the carriages were hauled on their $3\frac{1}{2}$ mile route by cable before steam-engines took over. Slip-coaches operated on a number of railways way back in the nineteenth century and well into the twentieth.

Some passengers might have heard about guard Bill Cordly of Birmingham. You can imagine his discomfort when, on one or two occasions, he misjudged the braking of his slip-coach at Hatton, near Warwick, and it stopped about a hundred yards short of the station. For the convenience of the passengers, the stationmaster suggested that perhaps it would be better to put the station itself on wheels.

Even worse: the guard of the slip-coach on the 6.35 p.m. from Paddington slipped the rear coach prematurely that should have stopped at Reading. Instead, it came to rest in the dark, in the deep two-mile Sonning cutting. Terrified lest they should be struck by another train from the back, passengers had to wait for forty minutes until an engine arrived to rescue them. That happened on 7 March 1927.

It is surprising that slip-coaches continued to be used right up to 1960. The last one in Britain was to run on 9 September 1960 on the 5.10 p.m. express from Paddington to Wolverhampton, the rear carriage being slipped off at Bicester.

A colleague in the Bletchley area named Horace Murray held a steady position as a relief clerk at goods stations. Many goods stations at the smaller places came under the control of the stationmaster, whose full title was stationmaster and goods agent.

As a relief man, Horace travelled most of the time within a fairly wide area. I often saw him getting on or off a train, carrying an attaché case. It was small enough to be acceptable by official prying eyes, yet large enough for Horace to carry stocks of chocolates and cigarettes at cut prices. He seemed to have assembled a solid and regular clientele as the basis of his pecuniary enterprise. Even with only a penny or so off the shop prices, he could build a good following.

He called on me for a friendly chat while I was acting stationmaster at Fenny Stratford, just one mile from Bletchley station on the Bedford line. It was shortly after I had married. I placed him at about forty. He usually wore a bowler hat and quiet dark suit, and he spoke with a Buckinghamshire accent. Always a happy smile on his ruddy face. I hadn't yet discovered the extent of his commercial enterprises.

'Horace,' I asked, 'd'you know where I can order half a ton of coal?'

'My dear chap, this is your lucky day. I know just the man. Joe Blackton. Coal-merchant in the High Street. It'll cost you 27 shillings.'

'Oh, thanks. I'll call on him tomorrow.'

A wicked expression crept over his face. 'But I know another bloke who'll do it for less.'

'How much less?'

'Three bob. That brings it down to twenty-four bob.'

'Same quality?'

'Exactly the same.'

'Ah, who's that bloke, Horace?'

His face sparkled into a brilliant and happy smile. 'You're talking to him. In person.'

'Good heavens! You're serious?'

He laughed at my surprise. 'I'm dead serious.' He laughed again. 'You call at my house in the Bletchley Road this evening and I'll book your order. If you want, I can fix delivery for tomorrow.'

'It's a deal.'

With that, he hurried to catch the push-and-pull steam train that had just run into the platform. He was off to work at Bedford goods depot for the day where, if I'm any judge, he'd flog a few packets of cigarettes and chocolates.

The following week I was still at Fenny Stratford, a detail that Horace had already checked with me. He called in the booking-office, where I was alone. From his inside jacket he produced a great fat wad of paper money and his LMS savings bank deposit book.

He said, 'I don't want the regular stationmaster to know about this lot. Will you bank it for me?'

'Yes, of course, Horace. It's a pleasure.'

I was tempted to make some comment just to provoke him, but restrained the impulse. Meanwhile, I counted the money to make an entry in his deposit book. My wicked and furtive and curious eye swept around the two open pages in those few seconds during which I slowly, oh, so slowly, made the necessary entry. I was dazzled to see such impressive deposits made from time to time. I handed the book back to him, deadpan.

I had no idea why he didn't want the regular stationmaster to know about his personal bank account. My task would be to bank it locally with Lloyd's along with the station cash. I knew it would be credited to Horace's account within a few days. He would earn on it interest at $2\frac{1}{2}$ per cent, which was about the going rate for similar savings accounts.

Before he left, I reminded him, 'You know, there's a vacancy up the line for a goods agent. It should be right up your street.'

'Not me, Frank. It's only a small place and I'd lose most of my private customers. In strict confidence, mind you.'

'I understand. I'd feel the same in your position.'

'Besides, I've got six mouths to feed. My wife, three daughters, a pet goat and a talking parrot!'

He dived deeply into his suitcase, took out a large bar of Cadbury's nut and fruit chocolate, my favourite. His face was alight. 'Have this one on me!' And he was gone.

Talking about moonlighting, there was far more scope in the coalfields in the north-east of England, and it was official. The London & North Eastern Railway positively allowed some of their stationmasters to moonlight by day, despite Rule 1 in the standard Rule Book stating explicitly, 'Railway servants must not engage in trade.' It happened in North Yorkshire, Durham and Northumberland.

The stationmaster, of course, earned a commission on any sales he achieved. Local coal-merchants took delivery of wagons of coal from the collieries. This they deposited in fenced areas in the railway station goods yards. From these stocks, the merchants would load coal into horse-drawn carts and in motor lorries for local deliveries to their customers. Here's where the astute middle man, the stationmaster, stepped in. He would secure orders and pass them on to the merchant of his choice, if several used his station yard.

The collieries had seen that the local stationmaster was ideally placed to look after the interests of the local coal-merchants. Collieries were great users of the railways, and railway managements were happy to go along with it.

My friend and colleague Philip Wilson, who worked in the north-east, was told by his stationmaster, 'I want you to look after any load of coal that goes over the weighbridge. However busy you are in the office, get there sharpish.'

Philip, who was no yes-man, objected: 'When I'm in the booking-office, that's my first job. I must look after passengers first. It's they who pay my wages!'

Grunting and growling, the stationmaster mooched off. He knew full well Philip was right. He was just trying it on.

Of the stationmasters who did this coal-agency work, one of them in time was earning more from his coal commission than from his railway salary. Eventually he left the railway to become a full-time coal agent. Just before he left, he invited one of his booking-clerks to walk up Station Road with him.

'You see that lovely house, me lad? It's mine. All paid for out of my coal commissions!'

In my early years in steam railways, I came across quite a number of railwaymen who did moonlighting jobs. For people who worked shifts on branch lines, a range of openings could be found. Smallholdings were popular. The man would sell fruit and vegetables, and eggs too if he kept hens. Household painting and decorating suited men on shift work. A shunter I knew did well in hair-cutting. He charged 2d. for boys and 3d. for men. The going rate at the barber's was at least a penny more.

I did a bit of moonlighting myself, but it will come in a much later chapter.

8

No Way to Treat a Gold-braid Cap

When the stationmaster at Islip (on the Bletchley-Oxford line) was promoted elsewhere, I filled the gap for several weeks in the summer. I found Islip a charming old village in rich brown stone, complete with village store-cum-post office, a butcher's shop, a few rustic pubs and a fine old church standing square-towered and high in the village square.

In my leisure hours I visited Oxford, city of dreaming spires, six miles away, and I gazed in admiration at the magnificent architecture of the colleges' wandered down the High, sank a pint at the Mitre, punted on the Cherwell and enjoyed my proper insignificance in that ancient seat of knowledge and learning. Little did I realize then as a single man that one day one of my own sons would gain a scholarship to enter the university.

When the trains came into the station, I found it an odd name to call out to the few passengers who might be alighting. I first called it Islip to rhyme with 'fizz', but Albert Eveson, the elderly porter, quickly corrected me. 'It should be Islip like in ice cream.'

Mr George Harris, a youngish local farmer, lived half a mile from Islip. On most days of the week he despatched a few churns of milk, carried in the guard's van, their destination being one of the big dairy companies. One of the most pleasant moments in my daily routine was to hear the clip-clop of Farmer Harris's horse and the clanking of the milk churns on the cart as it approached the station in the morning sun.

If Lucy, the station cat, garbed in stripy marmalade, was around, she would tear off in fear. Why, I know not. Perhaps it was the rattle of the churns, or the smell of pigs which George Harris carried around with him like a proud, enveloping aura. Lucy proved useful for keeping down the

95

mice population in the storeroom where we sometimes heaped sacks of grain for our farming customers. At the time I spent there, she was suckling four pretty little kittens. Like their mother, they were dressed fashionably in striped marmalade. When they weren't feeding or sleeping, they mewed and played around together.

This particular morning the farmer was a little late for the 8.15 a.m. train to Oxford. I heard the engine whistle in the far distance as it rounded the curve coming from Bicester. At the same time, the horse and cart loaded with milk churns came rattling down the road to the station, with George in command of the reins from the driving seat and bellowing, 'Get on there, Dobbin!'

Porter Albert Eveson and I were fascinated as we watched the frantic race between the steaming iron horse and the frothing horse-flesh horse. Noises of the approaching train competed for our hearing against the cart of clanking milk churns. The scene took me right back to boyhood days when I read *Ben Hur*, a thrilling story about a race between Roman gladiators in their speeding chariots. (I fancy it was a juvenile version written by Arthur Ransome in the *Children's Newspaper*.) Now, first in the station was the train. A few people climbed aboard. With a knowing smile and a wink, the driver leaned out of his cab.

Albert, the porter, said, 'I better give farmer an 'and.'

Farmer George Harris's face flushed into one wide grin. 'Thought we'd never make it!'

I assured him, 'We would have held the train for you, wouldn't we!'

With expert handling, the farmer lowered the churns one by one to the ground; then, with a deft turn of the wrist, he rolled each one on its bottom rim to the nearby guard's van. A few schoolboys who had joined the train watched the operations. The guard also lent a hand. Four churns had been loaded into the van, and the farmer was rolling out the last one. Just as he reached the guard's van he slipped and about a gallon of pure white liquid spilled out onto the platform.

'Oh, blast!' he grunted like one of his pigs, in a sound that went with his personal smell. 'Let's hope them dairy nobs don't notice.'

The schoolboys could be seen through the carriage windows snickering behind their hands.

With a blow of his whistle and a wave of his flag, the guard signalled the train away. Soon it steamed off under the bridge and was out of sight.

Hot and sweaty, Farmer Harris sprawled out onto a platform seat and mopped his brow with a khaki handkerchief. Then along darted Lucy, and in seconds she was laying into the tempting liquid like nobody's business. I noticed she was careful to lap at the edges and keep her feet on dry land, as it were.

Within a minute, along scampered four furry little bundles of fresh marmalade, took the cue from their mother, then waded in, wet feet or not. It was a memorable sight, and the three of us laughed with the sheer pleasure of watching their charming antics. When they had had their fill, they all trotted back to the storeroom, mother leading, and spent happy hours cleaning themselves up.

Two days later came another load of milk churns just as the train ran into the platform. It must have been the familiar clanking of the churns that attracted Lucy, for she came bounding up and watched eagerly as each churn was loaded into the guard's van. Soon four little kittens came scampering along expectantly. Lucy herself followed closely behind the farmer's heels wherever he moved. One of the schoolboys getting into a compartment said with a cheeky expression, 'Who said cats aren't intelligent!'

From that day on, Lucy always came to greet the farmer whom she had previously feared. She would caress his ankles with her furry face, mewing plaintively and cocking an eye on each churn as it was handled. Hopefully, of course.

Back at Islip for a short spell in the late autumn, one of my jobs was to light the four oil-lamps on each of the two platforms. In windy weather it was far from funny. I was surprised that the stores people at HQ did not complain about the quantity of matches I ordered. I also needed to light the oil-lamps in the booking-office and in the booking-hall, and my handlamp which could be turned to show red, green or white. My predecessors must have been doing this chore for nearly a century. Oil-lighting did not make your bookwork and accounts too easy. It reminded me of childhood visits to relations in the country whose only source of lighting was oil-lamps.

At Islip our only source of water, including that for the stationmaster's house, was from a hand-pump in an adjacent shed. You always knew when it was bath night at the gaffer's house, for he and his wife would trundle nearly a hundred yards in turns, pumping and carrying buckets of water which they put in the boiler to heat up. On a wet and windy night, they had to don their oilskins. Never once did I hear them grumble.

A couple of miles down the line towards Bicester was an occupation level crossing. It was used by the local farmer to get from one field to another, but there was no public road; hence the term 'occupation'. A small churn was used to get water to the level crossing. Poor old Joe, the keeper, didn't even have a pump. The churn was conveyed in the guard's van of the one daily goods train. The churn was collected empty on the way to Oxford, where it was filled with water, and delivered on its return for Bletchley. Not exactly gracious living.

One lunchtime my internal telephone rang. It was Joe. 'That goods 'as just gone through and he never stop wi' me water, Mr Ferno.' He never could get my awkward name right. 'The Missus is killing me. Her want her cup of tea. And so do me, mate. What about it?' Living in such an isolated spot, he depended upon his daily churn.

'I'll see if I can get a PW man to bring you a few gallons. As soon as he's on the way, I'll ring you. Don't worry, Joe. Tell your wife she'll get her tea soon.'

Enquiries revealed that a different guard had taken the return train back to Bletchley, which was unusual. And he had overlooked the water. I managed to persuade Jim Plant, a permanent-way man, to carry half a pail of water to keep Joe and his wife going until the next day.

There was another level crossing near Islip, but it was on the Oxford side and was lightly used by public transport. My friend and colleague Stanley Johnson, a district inspector, asked me to look out for a man to work at the crossing to replace one who was retiring.

I telephoned the ganger in charge of a team of platelayers based at Bicester. Walter Mopson, I believed, bore me a grudge for turning down one of his men he had recommended for fog signalling duties, but I had found the man weak in his knowledge of the requisite rules. However, seeing the ganger along the track, I now asked him, 'Any of your chaps interested in a crossing-keeper's job at Islip, Walter?'

'Might be.'

'There's a cottage to go with the job.'

Walter looked thoughtful. Then his suntanned face screwed itself up into a twisted smile. 'Well, now. Yes, I reckon Uriah Lunt would take to that job. He's married with some kids. Used to be a farm labourer up at the Grange. Bin with us these four year. He know a bit about the railroad.'

'That's just fine, Walter. By the way, I seem to remember you and I had a bit of a difference of opinion that last time we met. But I appreciate your advice on this one.'

'That be all right, mister. Let's hope us'll be good friends after he's taken the job on.' Again, that twisted grin. I couldn't make it out. Something funny here, I thought. But I can't put my finger on it.

Walter added, 'I be a-sending him up to your office s'afternoon.'

As arranged, Uriah turned up. Early fifties, a fat man with thick matted hair, a great walrus moustache and a sallow complexion. Supporting his cord trousers was a heavy leather belt over which liberally bulged a large piece of belly.

'That railroad cottage. Do us good. We'm only got a little place wi' a thatched roof up at the Grange.'

'Right, Uriah. I'll tell the inspector, and he will come to see you and fix you up with the job. But he makes the final decision.'

'Thank ee kindly, sir. Me missus and kids'll like the crossing. You be a proper genlman, sir, that you be. I'll do me best in that there job. Me very best.'

Some months later, I travelled with Inspector Johnson on a train from Oxford bound for Bletchley. Within a few minutes we were passing the Islip public level crossing, several hundred yards before reaching the station.

Mr Johnson gave me an odd grin – and pointed through the window of the carriage. 'See those little wooden huts in the crossing-keeper's garden?'

'Oh, yes. What are they for, hens, rabbits, dogs?'

'No. You remember Uriah Lunt? Well, I took him through the rules for working the crossing. There's very little traffic over it. Just a few farmers' carts. We got all that worked out. Then I made my recommendation to Derby HQ, who agreed it. All we had to fix then was to get his furniture in.'

'Sounds simple enough.'

'Sure. We'd fixed all the paperwork, did the records, settled his wages and the lot.'

'So?'

'Then we find he's got sixteen kids!'

'Good heavens, what a shock!'

We were now travelling towards Bicester, the countryside drifting by and steam billowing from the engine. He looked at me sideways in a curious way. 'You're sure it is a shock to *you*?'

'Yes, of course it is. Absolutely. You don't think I'd play a trick like that on you, Stanley, do you?'

He suddenly looked more cheerful and reassured me. 'Of course not.'

'Now then, something comes back to me. The p-way ganger at Bicester recommended Uriah Lunt to me. The ganger and I had had a slight difference of opinion some months previously, and he gave me such a wicked smile when we were talking about Uriah Lunt. I remember feeling a bit suspicious, but I just couldn't put my finger on it.'

'I understand, Frank. Anyway, after we had appointed Lunt officially, we couldn't confess to headquarters that we'd made a balls of it, could we! So we had no option but to build those huts in his garden. We had to beat the immediate problem.'

Ah well, live and let live, eh?

One Monday morning, a horsey gentleman resplendent in loud check sports jacket, breeches and leggings and sporting highly polished brown shoes, called on me at Islip station. He wanted to send a racehorse to Newmarket on the Wednesday. Would I have a horsebox ready for the journey. I worked out the cost. He said he would give the money to the stable lad who would bring the horse to the station for the morning train, and travel with it in the special passenger compartment in the box itself.

Using the internal railway telegraph, I ordered a horsebox, complete with passenger compartment and partition. The stable lad would have a reasonably comfortable journey on his upholstered seat, and a partition was necessary to protect the lone horse from being jolted from one side of the horsebox to the other. Both the partition and the inner sides of the box would be padded in leather for the comfort of the horse.

I failed to mention to my gentlemanly customer that I was practically an equine ignoramus. In fact, this would be the first time I had had to see to the despatch of such a distinguished animal. I took his order as though I accepted half a dozen horses a week to be despatched to racecourses all round Britain, from Ascot to Aintree. The train, I explained, would leave at 8.40 a.m. and travel via Bletchley to Cambridge, the box changing there for Newmarket. I asked for the horse to arrive at my station about fifteen minutes before train departure time. Fifteen minutes was pure guesswork. I had no idea how long it would take to load the thing into the box, but I presumed the stable lad would know his stuff.

On Tuesday afternoon the empty horsebox arrived on the local goods train. On the Wednesday morning I was up bright and early and reached the station before eight. The brown-painted horsebox on four wheels was standing safely on the short piece of line that led to a small dock or platform that was partly fenced in. Meanwhile, in the booking-office I booked a few morning passengers bound for Oxford to the west, and towards Bletchley, Bedford or Cambridge to the east.

Dead on 8.25 a.m. I caught sight of a man leading a fine golden chestnut towards the station dock.

I joined him and greeted, 'Good morning!'

"Mornin' to you, sir. I brought Golden Beauty for the joyride.'

Stable lad? He was old enough to be my dad. He had fuzzy grey sideburns and a ruddy complexion in rich leather. His old brown jersey was tatty, and he wore a cloth cap over to one side.

Golden Beauty really was a magnificent animal, sleek and shining in that splendid colour. He was the sort of horse I could perhaps make a friend of. But at the moment he struck me as a little lively and excited in his strange surroundings.

I unfastened the drop door of the horsebox, which made a walk-way from the dock. I then secured the partition into position. With some difficulty the stable lad was trying to lead Golden Beauty towards the box, but he wasn't having any. He tossed his head vigorously and whinnied in loud protest. A few passengers had wandered along to the end of the station platform to get a closer view. I suppose they seldom shared a train journey with a racehorse. I began to feel anxious about the whole operation.

Any minute the train would arrive, and we hadn't even got the animal into the box. Indeed, I then heard a whistle from the engine as the train steamed into the station platform. At the shrill of the engine whistle, the horse properly took fright and stood on his hind legs and showed his teeth. The stable lad was holding on to the bridle like nobody's business and coaxing the horse in a quiet and unruffled manner.

In the mêlée, Golden Beauty knocked my gold-braided cap to the ground. Now the horse was quieter but I still kept my distance. He splayed his back legs out, stood as still as a statue and emptied his bowels. Most of the steaming pile dropped into my upturned cap. Excitement relieved, the horse was led by the stable lad quietly into the box. On the way, he trampled unceremoniously on my desecrated cap. Blast and damnation! My precious gold braid, new last month, really mucked up. Now I would have to order a new one, after awkward explanations. Who could blame the head of our clothing stores in Manchester for not believing a word of it!

Lifting the door that had formed a ramp was a two-man job. When it was in position as a door once more, the stable lad, who had fixed it firmly with its bolts, gave it a pat.

'That be nice and secure now, Mr Stationmaster. I be sorry about yourn cap. I hopes you'll get another.'

But his leathery face creased up into tell-tale amusement at my expense before he climbed into his lonely little compartment.

A few amused passengers who had witnessed my embarrassment had a smile or two as well, as they joined the train before it backed up to the horsebox which the guard coupled up to the train. The guard signalled the driver to start the engine, which was a large 2-6-4 tank type, often seen on the Oxford and Cambridge branches.

With a sigh, I found a short stick and used it to lift up my subverted headgear, which I deposited in the station dustbin.

Millbrook, between Bletchley and Bedford on the Cambridge branch, was my base the following week. Among my paperwork on the desk of my tiny private office was a circular from the district commercial office. It stated that on Wednesday afternoon an officer's special coach would be calling, as part of the district officer's annual tour of inspection of his domain. He would be accompanied by two or three of his senior assistants. Stationmasters were expected to be in attendance in full and correct uniform to greet the 'special', and here was I in a grey trilby hat in soft felt. To the district chief, it would spell Disrespect, with a capital D. Searching the cupboards in my office, I managed to find the gold-braided cap of the regular stationmaster. I put it on my head. It looked like a pimple on a haystack. Inside it, I found that it was a size $6\frac{1}{2}$ against my size seven. No good.

A telephone call from the signalman in the station box warned me that the special would arrive within a few minutes. As usual in the anticipated presence of the mighty, I felt the butterflies flutter. Ridiculous. But there it is. One day I'll get rid of the things.

On the platform I saw the 'special' approaching. It consisted of a 2-6-0 tank engine and one officers' special coach. That little unit was always known down the line as an officers' special, even if it had several coaches and a dining-car in the set. I knew that in addition to the officers would be a clerk to make essential notes and a dining-car steward to serve a light meal and wine.

The chief, with two of his henchmen, alighted and approached me, frowning. There was a hard edge to his voice. 'Ferneyhough, why are you improperly dressed? I presume you are the stationmaster!'

What do you do, tell the man the truth that seems like a fairy tale or tell him a fairy tale that seems like the truth?

'The truth is, sir, that a racehorse deposited a load of his own pure fertilizer into my uniform cap and then trampled it in.'

His two assistants had a job to keep straight faces. So did I.

But the chief was angry. 'You're a stupid fool, man! If you think you can trifle with me like that, you're very much mistaken. You let me have a full report about your missing cap. On my desk in Northampton tomorrow morning. Without fail!'

'I'll see to it, sir.'

He commanded, 'Now come with me.'

Three obedient shadows followed their leader beyond the end of the platform to the sidings and the goods shed (I served as stationmaster and goods agent). On the goods deck, the DO pointed to some bags of cattlecake. 'When did these arrive?'

'Yesterday afternoon, sir.'

'Does the farmer know?'

'Yes. I sent him a postcard.'

'What are these four empty wagons doing?'

'They're needed by the brickworks company for the despatch of bricks.'

'When?'

'First thing in the morning, sir.'

He even spotted a heap of new sleepers for the track, and he told me to find out from the engineer's department what they were for. They were nothing to do with my department and I had absolutely no responsibility for them. But it was safer to answer. 'Of course, sir.' And so it went on. They spent time in the booking and parcels offices but fortunately could find nothing to criticize. I couldn't help feeling that he was disappointed, and I don't like my district officers being disappointed.

He walked along the platform to our miniature plot of station garden and examined it hopefully. 'Get somebody to do some weeding. It's looking very untidy.'

With that final salvo he climbed into his official carriage, followed obediently by his two acolytes. His parting happy words to leave a cheerful atmosphere at my little station came out bitingly, 'See that you're properly dressed in future!'

When their short train had departed in a furious roar in a cloud of steam and smoke, Ted Appleton, the booking-clerk, came up to me with curiosity bursting out of him.

'What did you say, Mr Ferneyhough, to upset the old man?'

'The chief asked me a straight question – where was my uniform cap. And I gave him a straight, honest answer.'

'That seems innocent enough.'

'But he didn't believe me.'

I told Bill the story about the racehorse. His reaction was, 'I'm not surprised he didn't believe you!'

I gave him a wink. 'I should have told the old man an outright lie. A plausible one. It would have been much less trouble.'

I was a sweet innocent in this farrago between master and man. I reminded myself to cross the chief's name off my list of officials I had worked for who could help me in my future promotion.

9
Odd Goings-on at Cambridge

It was a wet autumn morning. I was in charge of Castle-thorpe station on the main line between Bletchley and Rugby. The telephone rang. 'Hallo, is that the station-master? Buckley Manor here. This is the butler speaking.'

'Oh, yes. Can I help you?'

I didn't say 'sir' to the butler; it didn't seem right. After all, I was a stationmaster, albeit of the very lowest rank. But I recognized instantly that his accent was far superior to my north Staffordshire lingo.

'The Squire would like the express to be stopped on Friday morning. He'll be going to London again.'

'Thank you. We'll be very glad to arrange it for the Squire. Goodbye.'

It sounded like a conversation from the nineteenth century. It could even be a hoax. Though hoaxes were very rare. Except in storybooks.

I hadn't the faintest idea what the butler was talking about, but I assumed it must be a regular arrangement of some sort. My total staff consisted of two porters, one on each shift, and three signalmen, one on each shift. I asked the porter, who also booked tickets for the passengers, kept the daily books, swept the platforms, swilled out the toilets, delivered parcels on the station bike in the village, did his football pools on Wednesdays and painted the platform edges white twice a year on a Thursday.

'Oh, yes,' he chuckled. 'Squire, he go to London every few month. We have to phone Bletchley Control, and then they phone the Rugby station gaffer what gives a stop order to the driver.'

'This is usual, then, eh, George?'

'Sure. They says to me it's an old agreement. Bin going on for centuries.'

When I telephoned Bletchley Control, they took the

message in their stride. It was the only example of its kind
that I ever dealt with personally.

On the appointed day, along with the butler I escorted the
Squire, who wore a bowler hat and a long black coat, to the
train. I opened the door of an empty first-class compartment
and, as my forelock was covered, touched my gold-braided
cap and said, 'Pleasant journey to you, sir.' I felt he was
entitled to the accolade, and he smiled in response. I had
never been smiled at by a genuine, 22-carat squire before,
and I can strongly recommend it.

He sank into the luxury of a corner seat and his butler
handed to him a highly polished briefcase in tan leather. The
driver acknowledged the guard's signal to start with a 'pop'
on his engine whistle, and the great train gathered itself into
thrusting mobility and rapidly gaining speed, headed south
for Euston.

Discreetly the butler followed me closely along the
platform, leaned towards me and said conspiratorially, in a
whisper that seemed to echo around the deserted station, 'A
gift for you, sir. Compliments of the Squire.' Notice, he said,
'sir'. Then he glided quickly and quietly away. I heard the
clip-clop of a horse's hooves and saw he was driving his
master's carriage.

In the privacy of my little office, highly curious, I opened
the hessian carrier-bag and discovered two fat rabbits. I
produced them rather as a conjuror does out of a top hat.
What the hell could a single chap do with two fat rabbits?

I later learned that when the railways were first being
built, many wealthy landowners would allow a line to cross
through their estates only if they could have some trains
stopped for them specially, and legal agreements were made
accordingly. Some of them continued in force until well into
the present century, and a few remained even after the
railway amalgamations of 1923. That at Castlethorpe was
one of them.

At many a country station, I am sure you can imagine the
stationmaster and his staff, all well brushed and polished,
welcoming the landed gentleman, his wife, children, a
servant or two and the family pet dog, and receiving in

return for their servile attention a brace of pheasants, a couple of rabbits or even a fat tip.

Back at Millbrook again, we had a racehorse to send to Southwell, the station serving the Southwell racecourse. It was to be despatched by a well-known horse-breeder. We had ordered a horsebox in good time. Two stable lads brought the animal, on a bridle, to the station at half past nine for the ten o'clock train.

At a quarter to ten the porter came round from the yard to my office in a sweat. 'She's kicking and shying like anything, gaffer. And time's getting on.'

My propensity for dealing with difficult racehorses was still strictly limited. When I reached the yard, I found the fiery animal making for the railway line and the two hefty stable lads hanging on grimly to the halter and trying to pat her neck. But she wasn't having any, and her sleek black coat was already wet and steamy from sweat. Thinking about that train getting nearer and nearer, I withdrew to a safer position. Every man to his last, I thought, but the last thing for me was to display my equine ignorance.

As they got her back into the yard and away from the dangers of the railway line, she was still shying and snorting. Then a small boy, aged about thirteen, in breeches and leggings came running up, not cheeky but really confident. 'I'll get her in for you, gents.'

One of the stable lads, in a phrase not too familiar to Sunday school teachers, said, 'Boy, you be off, quick!'

But the boy was insistent. I said, 'Give him a chance.'

While they tried to hold her still, the boy leaped up and mounted her, bareback. We stood around open-mouthed. The horse began to trot around the yard as the young rider confidently coaxed her, stroking her beautiful neck. They trotted round happily three times, the horse getting quieter each time. The fourth time she was walking sedately and, bending low on her neck, the boy rode her straight into the horsebox before a whip could say crack. What a relief!

After I had seen the train with its precious load away to Bedford, I asked the porter if he had learned anything about the boy, by now nowhere to be seen.

'Yes, Guv'nor. You know that little circus what come in yesterday. Well, he is one of them trick riders, you see.'

On the railway, it is fairly common to see a passenger miss his train by a few seconds. But we don't purposely give the 'right away' signal for a train to start if we see a late-comer charging up to the station in a panic. (Incidentally, although the guard is responsible for signalling the engine-driver to start, it is the duty of the senior man on the station platform first to give a signal to the guard. Although the guard is in charge of the train, the senior platform man is in charge of the station. In other words, a guard is not allowed to signal his train away until he has received a signal from the platform man. And the platform man is not allowed to give a signal to a driver until the guard has given his 'right away' signal. All very complicated. It's all in the Rule Book, even more complicated.)

However, the stationmaster at Woburn Sands on the Bletchley-Cambridge line had a slightly different approach to late-comers. A short train started from there at 8.45 a.m. to run the nine-minute journey of four miles to Bletchley, where it connected with a main-line train from Crewe to make a non-stop journey to London.

Woburn village, by the Duke of Bedford's estate, was the home of a handful of people who were 'something in the City'. Despite their obvious standing in the world, the stationmaster would walk into Station Road replete in smart uniform and, just before the train was due to start, blow his whistle, wave his arm impatiently and shout aloud to the last few stragglers, 'Hurry along there, gentlemen, please. This train's late already. Damn it, get a move on!'

The few late-comers were now used to this sort of treatment and ignored the fellow completely. They walked briskly in full regulation identification kit – City suits, bowler hats, umbrellas, briefcases, pink *Financial Times* tightly tucked under their arms, to join the waiting train. I had seen the performance several times during a few days' training I had had with the stationmaster, and it was a hard struggle to remain silent. These fellows were not going to run for anyone. My dear sir, it's just not done.

Unconcerned though these city gents appeared to be, hard things must have been said to somebody higher up on the LMS Railway, for the next I heard about our impatient stationmaster was that he had been promoted – to the post of goods agent near Coventry. I'm afraid he would find little use for his whistle in a goods office.

If a guard misses his train, ah that is a different matter. Some guards, especially the younger men, had the naughty habit of signalling their train away, then jumping into the guard's van as the train is gathering speed, rather like the fairground man who jumps onto the roundabouts. I have often watched a guard a little anxiously as once again he has just about made it.

During the gap between the stationmaster moving to the Midlands and a new one taking his place, I worked for a few weeks in charge at Woburn Sands. I was seeing away a mid-morning train, semi-fast from Cambridge, moving off for Bletchley from whence it would continue to Oxford. Suddenly I became aware of a scurrying on the platform, and it was an amusing sight as the guard ran alongside his train, trying to get into his van.

Just as he reached it, he collided with a teenage girl who was waving off her boyfriend, and they fell together in a heap on the platform. I blew my whistle and waved towards the engine, but all to no avail. It was now steaming away in a great flurry of billowing smoke and steam.

I helped the two of them to their feet and, as soon as the girl was out of hearing, the guard swore furiously in vexatious frustration. Frankly, I had to laugh at the fellow. Standing there with his green flag held impotently in his hand, he looked so forlorn and lonely without his train, which, by now, had vanished into the meadows and woods.

I telephoned Bletchley control office. They would arrange for a relief guard at Bletchley to take over the train for its forward journey to Oxford. The controller told me an engine and a goods brake van would be through Woburn Sands shortly, and I stood on the platform with the guard until the E & B came into the station. As the passenger guard climbed aboard the goods brake van to join the goods guard, he grinned broadly over his shoulder. 'I reckon I'll just have to slum it in this old wooden box on wheels!'

More seriously, when the guard had missed his train, the fireman should have been looking back. The train could then have been stopped for the guard to climb aboard. But obviously he wasn't watching. Yes, there was a rule for it, number 40. It stated clearly, 'When starting, the fireman must look back to see the whole of the train is following in a safe and proper manner, and to observe any signal that may be given by the station staff or guard.'

I visualized the procedure to be observed at Bletchley. When I telephoned the control office about the irregularity, the controller would secure the services of another guard to take the train to Oxford and would make a written note in the logbook. This is scrutinized daily by the district controller in person. He would have the guard call in his private office for a reprimand, which would be recorded. He would also have a memo sent to the engine shedmaster, who would deal suitably with the careless fireman, and that would end the matter.

I record an incredible incident. But first, the background. When foot-and-mouth disease struck in Cambridgeshire in the late thirties, hundreds of cattle and sheep had to be slaughtered and buried in lime pits. Farmers lost a great deal of money. Ordered by the Minister of Agriculture, the usual well-proved precautions were taken to contain the ravaging disease.

While acting as senior clerk at the LMS booking-office at Cambridge station, which the LMS shared with the LNER, I saw the official orders from the Ministry. British railways also issued special instructions to all stations concerning the movement of livestock into or out of infected areas in strictly controlled operations. This is a procedure I have often been involved with when working at country stations. For cattle-farmers, an outbreak can be catastrophic, and it had happened in Cambridgeshire before.

A Cambridge friend named George Wilde, employed at the Ministry, filled me in with some of the details of a shocking episode which occurred as the epidemic was just over its peak. At Cambridge station a neatly dressed young man, wearing an official armband and clutching a clipboard, along with two companions carrying large plastic bags, boarded the mid-morning semi-fast train about ten minutes before its due departure for London. They passed along the corridors of the sparsely occupied carriages and spoke to the passengers in turn.

Smiling, Mr Clipboard said, 'Sorry to bother you, folks. This awful foot-and-mouth business could be nearly over, thank heavens, but some precautions are still necessary, I'm afraid.'

In the compartment were mumbles of agreement. One or two stared through the window at the busy platform. The young man continued, 'Now, this is purely voluntary. If you'd let me have your shoes, we are treating the soles with disinfectant in the guard's van. You'll have them back in a very short time. Long before you reach London.'

A well-dressed gentleman in a corner seat asked, 'Pardon me, but have you any authority, a card or something?'

'Yes, of course, sir. Let me see if I can find it.' And he proffered a short letter on LMS Railway headed paper.

As the passenger's eye fell on the letter, the young man asked, 'Excuse me, sir. Are you a farmer?'

'No. But my people are, and they've had a bad time.'

'I'm very sorry, sir.' He retrieved his letter.

A rugged farmer type began to undo his bootlaces. 'It's a good idea, young feller. You can't be too careful. You're welcome to mine. I'm off to the Ministry to talk about my claim. I've lost a score of my best beasts. It's terrible!'

Along the train, others followed suit. The two plastic bags soon began to bulge. Pretty girls with elegant legs giggled and no doubt thought it no end of a lark, but elderly ladies seemed less enthusiastic.

Just before the train was due to start, the three young men hurried along the corridors. They emptied the shoes into a small heap on the floor of the guard's van along with parcels and mail bags, then briskly alighted onto the platform.

Nearby the guard was standing, with green flag and

whistle poised, keenly scanning the train before signalling it to start. The signal at the front end of the platform already showed green. He eyed the young men curiously. Mr Clipboard told him confidently, 'They're all ready now, guard. All yours.'

Only half listening, he mumbled, 'Eh? What? What's all mine, mister?'

'The shoes, guard. For the disinfectant. Foot-and-mouth, you know.'

'I don't know nothing about any shoes. What shoes?'

'The shoes. Passengers' shoes. You know, this foot-and-mouth outbreak.'

'Oh! Oh, yes. The shoes.'

He was obviously still concentrating on getting his train away on time. He added, a little absently, 'Leave it to me, laddie. I'll look into it after we move off.' Then he gave the signal to start, leaving the station momentarily empty and quiet.

As the train steamed along, all grace and power, from the great platform, famous for its exceptional length, a load of mostly shoeless passengers sat, a little self-consciously, talking and laughing. Probably this was their most friendly, happy railway journey since the day the war had ended in 1918. Nothing, just nothing, breaks down the traditional English reserve in a railway carriage so completely as sitting there without your shoes. And wondering when the hell you're going to see them again. Perhaps, as mile after pretty mile of tranquil English scenery flashed past the windows, some would begin to feel a little uneasy.

Meanwhile, in the guard's van, as the train rattled and roared along at a gathering pace, a puzzled uniformed official removed his peaked cap, emblazoned 'Guard' in smart lettering, and mopped his brow with a red spotted handkerchief. Scowling angrily at the heap of various kinds of footwear, he tripped over them as he moved to his seat. In a sudden fit of temper, he grabbed a shoe and flung it through the window. He then realized that his train was running through Shelford station. 'Oh, God,' he muttered. 'That shoe. I hope the bloody thing didn't hit anybody!' He never seemed to give a thought to the unfortunate owner.

He tidied up the pile of shoes and mumbled, 'Something funny going on here. The station gaffer at Liverpool Street will have to sort this lot out.' He moved a few parcels ready for unloading, then walked along the corridor to find out from the passengers what it was all about.

Meanwhile, back on the station platform at Cambridge, three neatly dressed, earnest young men, led by the most earnest-looking of them all still clutching his clipboard, solemnly approached the ticket-barrier. They handed their platform tickets to a sharp-eyed ticket-collector and ambled leisurely into Station Road.

As soon as they were well clear of the station buildings, they exploded into hysterical laughter. Tears rolled down their brightly flushed cheeks. Their stomach muscles must have ached unbearably. A few passers-by stopped and stared, wondering what all the excitement was about. Then, recovering, the team set off to stroll nonchalantly and happily back to their college, no doubt to regale their fellows with tales of their latest hoax.

And yet ...

Unbeknown to them, they had been followed by that sharp-eyed ticket-collector. Most politely and very firmly indeed, he badgered them for their names and college. They tried to fob him off, outwit him, tie him up in verbal knots. Mr Clipboard led the semantics. 'My dear feller, you're sure it was us? We've not been near the station for weeks. And we certainly don't belong to any college.'

'Oh, you think I'm mistaken?'

'Yes, of course, dear chap. Now run along and collect a few more tickets.'

'I'm certainly not mistaken. I'm going to nail you boys. I'll nail you even if you doesn't speak another word. You see, sir, I knows you. Your pappa is one of our top nobs, and I knows him as well. It's no good you wasting your time denying it, sir.'

Sharp-eyed? That ticket-collector was very determined, too. I like to believe that those undergraduates were pressed to pay for damages and to be suitably dealt with as well.

10
Do Rail Statistics Tell a Lie?

Why do most of us grouse about the boss most of the time –
that is, unless he pays us a rise or even a handsome
compliment? In the railway hierarchy, as in any other
pyramid structure, it starts at the bottom – say, the porter or
lowest-grade clerk, then the stationmaster or other local
supervisor, the district officer, the divisional superintendent,
the general manager, the chairman, the Minister of
Transport, the Prime Minister, then Parliament and finally
the voter, that's you and me.

These were my thoughts when I was promoted to be a
branch-line controller in the district control office at
Bletchley. Our job as a team, working three shifts of six in
each team, day and night, weekends, bank holidays, even
Christmas Day, was to regulate all the train movements,
passenger and goods, throughout our district.

Our territory covered the main line between Tring and
Rugby, the line through Northampton, and branches
including Oxford, Cambridge, Aylesbury, Luton, Towces-
ter, Peterborough, Banbury and a few others. Our chiefs
consisted of the district controller, his deputy, several
inspectors and a chief clerk.

A few years ago I felt scared of the very idea of being a
traffic-controller, and here it was – happening. I had a
week's training on each shift, then I was on my own. I won't
detain you with the few nightmares I suffered in those early
days, except for just one. During a night shift, when all my
colleagues were engrossed with their own telephoning, I
answered a call from the signalman at Bletchley number one
box on the main line. He told me, 'I've got the down express
from Euston coming, and there's a goods train running away
off the Oxford branch.'

'Put your signals to danger. Quick!'

'I can't. They won't work. All the levers are stuck.'

'Hang on, George. I'll ask the head controller.'

I rushed across to him, but he shushed me away. He was too busy. He'd got a runaway train at Northampton. I tore out onto the platform and saw the express approaching at the same time as the goods from the branch. They crashed and caught fire, engine whistles screaming.

Someone was shaking my shoulder and shouting at me. 'Wake up, Wake up! You're screaming!' It was my wife, Joan.

Perhaps this portrays the initial strain of life in the control office. But I conquered the job eventually and really enjoyed it no end.

In our traffic control room were large diagrams showing the entire district – lines, stations, engine sheds, sidings, signal-boxes, shunting-yards and the like. By the nature of the job, we had to give orders and instructions firmly and unequivocally. Wit and humour, banter and legpull, and plenty of tact were the principal manipulative ingredients to keep the wheels turning pretty happily. It was a help, of course, if you knew your job. My experience as a relief stationmaster in the district proved enormously useful. It must have been a factor in my appointment.

Down the line we were known as 'the brains department', or just 'the brains'. A yard foreman would say to his shunter, 'The brains tell me we've got to get them empties away afore midnight' or 'Ask the brains. It's their job, not ours.'

Drivers always enjoyed a laugh at the expense of their friendly enemies, the traffic-controllers. I heard Percy Parker tell this tale in the pub time and again. On each occasion it gathered a little more moss. He was the driver on a night goods train, and at two o'clock in the morning his engine failed. The pipe connection between the dome on top of the boiler which holds the 'driest' and most concentrated steam and the regulator, a sort of accelerator controlling the power, had become faulty. The regulator, therefore, was useless, known by footplatemen as 'lost' – in a word, inoperative, rather like a car accelerator becoming disconnected and the petrol tank empty.

Percy tells the yarn: 'I leaves me fireman on the engine, and I make my way in the dark with my handlamp. I gets to the signalbox. I rings the brains. And I tell 'em I need another engine.

'The brains says, "What's the trouble, driver?"

'And I says, "I lost me regulator."

'And he says, "Oh, er ... Your regulator. You've lost it. So you've lost your regulator have you, driver?"

' "I just said so!"

' "We haven't a spare engine just now. Can't you manage without your regulator?"

' "What you talking about, mister?"

' "Well, let me see, er ... There's not much traffic about now. Take your handlamp and look around. There's a good moon. You're sure to find it. Then call me back." '

As he finished his tale, Percy would slap his thigh with glee, and the lads would laugh uproariously.

'I've lost me regulator, I tells 'im. Tak your lamp and go look for it, he tells me. An' tak the moon wi' yer!' Then he would yell, 'Eh, lads, I've earned another pint!'

Among us railwaymen, shift working is endemic. We started our shifts at 6 a.m., 2 p.m. and 10 p.m. and we shared Sunday duties. I thus joined the ranks of other shift-workers – armed forces, police, fire services, medical, transport, gas, electricity, telephones, post, water supplies, the media, to quote more common ones. Without shift-workers, society would collapse – overnight!

At first, shift-working was fun. But only the fun of novelty. It soon wore off. Social life was dislocated. Bodily functions lost their rhythm. However, now that I was a householder, odd hours of free time had their domestic uses.

If a controller was sick, sometimes two of us had to work twelve hours each to cover the work. But changing duty at two in the morning was not screamingly funny, nor yet enchanting. Most of the gaps from absence were covered by a relief controller, poor devil!

Many shift-workers find daytime sleep a real nightmare. Doors bang. Dogs bark. Milk delivery is suddenly a cacophony of musical bottles bumping on concrete. A cheerful whistling schoolboy delivers misery along with the morning newspaper rattling through the letterbox. And there's the postman. Chattering children run and shout and bounce off to school. A neighbour hammers away at a faulty fence. A do-it-yourself fiend over the road makes holes in metal with an electric drill that whines and bores deep into your ears, sounding like a dentist's favourite instrument of torture. A car horn hoots. A lorry rumbles by. A neighbour's cockerel crows all day to show who's cock of his feathered harem. And now there is our new baby.

You lie there tossing and turning, shocked at your horrible imaginings of how to dispose of those noisy bodies who are smiting your sensitive eardrums. You feel you could compete with those thriller-writers who plot with diabolical relish their awful murders. Nightmares become daymares. As our semi-detached house was a mile from Bletchley station, at least my sleep would not be broken by my beloved steam trains.

'Try earplugs,' suggested my wife, ex-hospital nurse and highly qualified with her SRN to be an authority on such matters. 'Cottonwool with a smear of olive oil.'

She made a matching pair and plugged me in. We stood in the hall by the open door. I saw her lips move. I cupped hand to ear. She tried again, shouting loudly. 'Leave them in until I call you at teatime, my love.'

At the open door the surprised milkman thought we were having a shouting match, and he looked properly astonished, contemplating a couple not all that long married. To bed I went and slept like a top, whatever that is. My wife said, coyly, at teatime, 'I knew my long hospital training would come in useful one day!'

It worked all right. Yet being unable to hear properly left me feeling strangely vulnerable, as though to sudden danger. I felt a new sympathy for deaf people. But even they, with a hearing-aid, have an advantage. When bombarded by the boringly loquacious, they can always switch the fellow off.

Finishing work one early afternoon in the control office, I walked into near calamity. I went along Platform 8. Following my usual route, I would walk over a single-line siding, along a path, over a stile and into Bletchley Road for home. The lengthy alternative walk the other way was over the station bridge, right round the station and under the main railway bridge into Bletchley Road. Sometimes the single-line siding was occupied by a long train of wagons, blocking the way. Your options then were to walk the long way round or crawl under the wagons if they were standing still. Crawling under wagons? The Company's standard Rule Book strictly forbade any such foolhardiness.

This particular afternoon, wagons were in the siding. They were moving slowly. That told me something loud and clear. The wagons are attached to an engine. Then they stopped. As I reached the crossing place, I heard a frightened shout. Hurrying to the side of the wagons, I was astounded to see a young shunter named Tony Braybrook crouched in mud between the rails and under a wagon.

Panic-stricken, he called out. 'Eh, can you tell the driver to stop? I want to crawl out.'

'You can't crawl out yet, Tony. Stay put. Wait until the wagons are moved along the track.'

'Oh, dear God! I was mad to come this way. What shall I do?'

Possibly, if the locomotive shunted the wagons along the track, it would pass over Tony with all its heat and steam. Hot ash might drop on him, even a jet of seething steam could scald the fellow. Also, heavy couplings hanging from the wagons could easily strike his head unless he lay flat on the track. There's no doubt all these possibilities raced through his tormented mind. Slowly the wagons began to move, their wheels grinding on the dry rails.

Urgently I called to him. 'I'll get to the driver, then come back to you. Stay there. Lie down. Don't move! I'll be quick.'

As I hurriedly picked my way along the sidings to reach the engine, my mind was full of apprehension. I recalled my days in the accidents office at Derby HQ. Such things happened too often. Tony had two children and a good wife and home. How could he have been so idiotic? How could any of us, indeed!

It was a long raft of wagons. When I finally reached the

engine and told the driver, he said, 'Better tell Eddie. He's the shunter in charge.'

Eddie was angry. 'I've told 'im time and again. He could get a foot chopped off or summat. I'll tell driver to give two pops on his whistle, Mr Ferney. Then he can come out. And come and see me quick!'

It took a minute or so for me to reach Tony, by which time I heard two pops on the engine whistle. He crawled from under the wagons inch by inch in a very dejected state and covered in mud.

He muttered his thanks. 'It was terrible under there. All me life went afore me.'

He wasn't too pleased at having to report to his head shunter, but I gave him no option, even though he had signed off duty; no doubt he would get a strong ticking off.

I saw a porter one day cycling across the sleeper crossing at the ends of the eight platforms where trucks of parcels were trundled from one platform to another. There was no lift. The sleepers on the crossing were made up to the level of the rails. Of the eight lines of way, two were the fast ones, one in each direction. And believe you me, did those massive expresses belt along!

I called to the porter, whom I knew only slightly, and said in as friendly a way as I could, 'You're taking a big risk, you know.'

He dismounted from his bike and rounded on me. 'It's no business of yours, mate, what I bloody well do!'

I said no more and walked off. Because I'd mentioned it, it's just possible he would think quietly about it afterwards. I could have said, 'OK, get yourself bashed up by an express if you like. But somebody will have to go and tell your wife and kids!'

Somerset Maugham said somewhere that you can 'heal the sick and reform the wicked, but if a person is stupid, there's nothing you can do about it'. Except to remind ourselves that we all do daft things at times.

In his small corrugated iron cabin, a signal lampman was filling oil-lamps for the signals around Bletchley. He had a bench to work on, and outside the cabin rested an oil drum.

The cabin itself stood well away from other buildings and structures. One day, by careless handling he set fire to the place. He dashed through the door hell for leather, just in time to get out of reach of the oil drum that had exploded. Each incident of this kind brought improvements to working arrangements.

Apart from the standard Rule Book, the LMS headquarters regularly issued circulars to the staff on all aspects of safety. They ran poster campaigns and held staff meetings about safety. Men who took unnecessary risks, to themselves or railway property, were disciplined. For more serious accidents, at the Ministry of Transport was a vigorous railway inspectorate in which details of serious accidents were examined in public and their findings also made public. Faults or errors of staff, management or materials were firmly dealt with.

From my early days in the goods shunting yard at Hanley, then in the locomotive works offices for a stint at Crewe, and now as a branch-line controller for the Bletchley area, one thing was drilled into my very bones. A steam-locomotive is a very expensive animal to run. Maybe that is why 'it' is translated from the neuter gender to 'she'!

She has an expensive appetite for the best-quality solid fuel and a continuous venal thirst for soft water which must be regularly assuaged, otherwise she'll just blow her top. Then there is much cosseting and titivating, so that when she goes out on public view she looks really smart, making her 'escort' – if drivers will forgive the sobriquet – proud.

In the district office we compiled statistics, revealing the productivity of engines, firemen, guards, carriages, wagons.

Take goods engines. An engine is doing its best work during the hours it is hauling a full train of wagons of revenue-earning goods at a fair speed. But other work has to be done which is dead loss. Taking empty wagons to collieries, gasworks, power-stations, ironworks and such like. Pulling a breakdown train to a derailment. Conveying railway workers' trains to maintenance jobs or new installations, or just hanging around the sidings doing nothing except smoke. Naturally the bosses frowned on engines in steam standing idle.

One set of statistics we compiled for headquarters was 'Average number of wagons per goods train'. A high average saw our new chief, the district controller, Mr Becket, preening himself in self-satisfaction. A consistently low average would see him tearing his remaining hair in rage. It would also bring a man from headquarters travelling first class, wearing a sombre suit and Homburg hat, scuttling to the scene of disaster to see what we'd all been up to.

Let us switch now to the train control office itself. In a team of six on the afternoon shift, I am the branch controller. Around five o'clock I receive a phone call from the stationmaster at Potton. It is twenty-eight miles distant, in agricultural country, on the Cambridge line. I know John Littler, the gaffer there.

'Hallo, Control? Van of veg for London ready in an hour. Anything moving this way, Frank?'

I scan the diagram board with its movable tickets showing where all the goods trains are. I'm expected to know the passenger trains off by heart.

'Yes, John. We're in luck. E and B coming up from Cambridge towards six. I'll phone Cambridge and tell the guard. And your bobby can have him stopped at your sidings to pick up the van.'

'Fine. I've promised the farmer that his load of turnips will be at the market well before four in the morning.'

'OK, John. Should be easy. I'll follow through.'

An hour later his signalman called me. 'E and B and one van away at six-ten.'

On arrival at Bletchley, the van is detached and placed in the sidings. With other wagons and vans, it is shunted onto the night goods to London, and the turnips should be selling in Covent Garden before five the next morning. When handing over at ten o'clock to my night colleague, along with various other operating movements, I gave him details of the turnips and he would follow the load through to London. I signed off.

The same scene two weeks later. Mr Becket, the district

controller, sends for me. His private office is a few yards along Platform 8. When the boss sends for you, your stomach begins to churn up, and you wonder anxiously what you've done wrong. Why else would the boss send for you? As I enter, he is frowning over a batch of papers. He looks up with a smile, the smile of the tiger – with his mouth but not his eyes. Clean-shaven, greying, thinning hair and grey-suited, he is a biggish man in his fifties.

'Ferneyhough, you picked up a van of vegetables at Potton last Tuesday week.'

'I did indeed, sir.'

Could this be congratulations from the mighty on a nice piece of operation by an ambitious young controller of drive and fecundity? A veritable cornucopia of praise, in fact?

The smile from the mighty suddenly vanishes. 'You made an error of judgement. You shouldn't have done that.'

What a shock! Don't, I warn myself, fall into the trap again of arguing with the boss. He can make or break your career. Yet in all honesty I couldn't let this one go by without knowing why.

'There was a van of vegetables, sir. Turnips ...'

'Turnips or coconuts is irrelevant!'

'They were for next morning's market. Covent Garden. That van just had to connect with our night goods to London, otherwise there could have been a claim from the farmer.'

'I see. Go on.'

'I did the only thing possible, sir. I stopped an engine and brake that was doing no work and gave it the job of hauling a van of revenue-earning turnips.'

'Damn the turnips! But that's not the point, man. The point is this. An engine and brake van do not count as a train for the statistics. But an engine, a vanload of vegetables and a goods brake van do count as a train.' I could see he was getting angry. 'That so-called train of yours had only one wagon. And that one-wagon train damaged our average of number of wagons per train carried for the week. It damaged our statistics. Bad for the reputation of the district.'

Were my ears deceiving me? You could have knocked me down with an iron coupling-link, even a small one. Such dialectics would defy the mighty intellect of Pythagoras and could ruin the LMS Railway Company fast. Maybe I'd missed a point or two along the line.

'I believe, sir, that I did the only sensible thing. That engine and brake ...'

He snapped as I stood there, 'Don't let it happen again!'

'You are saying, sir, that the statistics for HQ are more important than the service to customers?'

In measured tones, he fairly shouts. 'Enough! That ... will ... be ... all!'

In disbelief I glare at him and stamp out through the door. I feel all boiled up inside and am breathing heavily. Still, I suppose the boss is the boss, so why argue? Do as the man says, even if it's barmy. Don't get emotionally involved. Enjoy yourself, even if it wastes the LMS Company's money. The shareholders won't know.

To cool down, I walk the length of the platform twice, then return to my desk in the control office. Tantalizing thoughts run through my head. Such as – I was absolutely right and should have stood my ground. I could have challenged him, 'Would you put it in writing, Mr Becket, sir, that your statistics count more than service to the customer?'

To which he could have replied, 'Your view, my lad, is limited to the day-to-day working. Mine is the broader view. Managing the whole district and how it fits into the entire LMS system. And whether you like it or not, understand it or not, HQ policy is strongly influenced by the statistics from districts such as ours.'

I could counter, 'Are you prepared to display a notice on the control office noticeboard, sir, describing what I did and stating that it must not be repeated, in case it damages the district statistics?'

Next could follow his devastating masterstroke. 'I would remind you, Ferneyhough, that Rule One in the LMS Rule Book states that, "All employees must pay prompt obedience to persons placed in authority over them." I'd also remind you, young man, that control work is a team job. My next report to HQ about your personal progress has to assess your ability to co-operate and to carry out the instructions of your superior officer ...'

In this particular case, when John Littler, the station-master at Potton, first made his request, I could easily have tossed it into the lap of my head controller and asked, 'What shall I do?' But I didn't, because the best and only way was obvious. What a frustrating odyssey to be sure! Then a happy thought struck me – maybe one day I'll become a district controller.

Unexpectedly, two months later I received a personal letter from the district officer. It said that I had been selected for promotion to a relief stationmaster's post based in Nottinghamshire. It left me with an enigma. I could never be sure whether Mr Becket had recommended me for the post to get me off his district or because he considered me worthy of more responsibility. Wouldn't it be boring to know the answers to all these trivial questions!

Working in the Bletchley area had been exciting, and enlightening about the working of the railway. Relationships with colleagues were friendly and helpful, with plenty of laughter on the way. Now, long years afterwards, those old friends are like mysterious shadows flickering on the walls of time. And what a pleasure it is on those fairly rare occasions when I happen to meet one of them again.

11
Nothing but a Load of Bull

Mansfield is my new base. It stands on the line between Nottingham and Worksop. In the north of the county, it is the centre of the coal industry, with ugly pyramids of slag oddly set in bucolic surroundings.

As a relief SM, I was expected to deputize for stationmasters, and others, up to two grades above my own grade four. When senior staff were in short supply, I occasionally moved to three grades above my own. As in the Bletchley area, I also deputized for several ranges of clerks, plus yardmasters when needed. Eventually I covered every clerical and admin job at Mansfield, a grade one station. I went from junior clerk to booking-clerk, senior booking-man, senior parcels man and stationmaster. You can imagine that one year working as a relief man brought far more experience of the railway ambience than working solely at one station and in the same post. In the top post I had the use of a pleasant private office, with the door labelled 'Stationmaster', a miniature holy of holies.

My moving up and down the scale of station staff encouraged Larry Clegg, one of the two station foremen who worked turn and turn about, to poke some familiar fun at my expense. I had turned thirty, and he was in his fifties, but we were good friends. In one particular week, when I deputized for the junior clerk in the booking-office, Larry Clegg greeted me at five in the morning on the early shift. He put on a commanding voice of authority and bellowed, 'Come on, boy. Get on with it!'

My response was meek, if mocking, as I touched my forelock. 'Yes, sir. Certainly, sir. Now, sir? Absolutely three bags full, sir!'

'Now, no cheek, lad. Remember you're talking to the station foreman himself.'

I thought, I'll get him for this. My chance is sure to come. Even if it takes six months. Sure enough, I was soon back at Mansfield, this time deputizing for the chief clerk, a dapper fellow who was most polite but a stickler for rules and regulations.

One of his weekly tasks was to draw a large sum of money from Lloyd's Bank to pay the wages. We drew about £1,000 (today equalling £40,000 or more). This job fell to me. On the day, I took George Baxter with me, the chief parcels clerk. We had a leisurely stroll of ten minutes to the bank, knocked on the door at nine o'clock, an hour before public opening time, then had good time to check all the cash without interruption.

Back at the office, behind locked doors, we spent two hours checking the money and putting it into numerous prepared wage-packets and tins. We paid the wages through a lift-up little door, at which a card hung: 'Wages paid 12 noon-1 p.m. and 2.30 p.m.-5 p.m. Large queues would assemble: men of every grade, including many drivers, firemen and cleaners from the engine sheds.

Meanwhile I was planning a minor embarrassment for station foreman Larry Clegg. He was particularly busy with trains coming in and out between noon and one o'clock and usually collected his wages, by special arrangement, at two when he signed off duty from the early shift.

George Baxter and I arranged to go out for lunch from 1.30 p.m. to 2.30 p.m. and leave Larry Clegg giving his fancy tap in code on the door of the empty pay office at two o'clock.

When we arrived back from lunch at 2.25 p.m., sure enough there was Larry with his bike, waiting for the pay door, still closed, to be lifted up. I opened it precisely at half past two.

Larry was a little put out. 'Eh, Mr Chief Clerk. What are you playing at? You know very well that I pick up me pay packet at two o'clock sharp when I'm on earlies.'

'Foreman, there are the times. Clearly on the card. Those are the chief clerk's laid-down rules.'

I gave him his packet, and he grinned widely. 'One up to

you, Mr Ferney. But I'll enter half an hour overtime for waiting.'

'And I shall cross it out with my chief clerk's blue pencil!' He suddenly looked serious. 'Oh, I've just thought of something.'

'What's that, Larry?'

'I'm saving it up for you. Good day!'

He certainly had me puzzled. He went off with his bike and made way for the queues of men behind him.

My week as chief clerk went by without incident. Trains with passengers and parcels, mailbags and bikes came in and out of the busy station, and Larry and I worked together in our usual amicable way. On the Monday I was sent off to Thurgarton for two weeks, a station between Nottingham and Newark on the Lincoln line.

With Mansfield being my 'home' station, I often saw Larry Clegg there in the course of my travels. We exchanged the usual pleasantries, and sometimes he would give a wicked and knowing grin as if he really had something up his sleeve.

Months later I was back at Mansfield again. The stationmaster was taking his two weeks' holiday leave. I had a staff numbering towards sixty. Several clerks, foremen, platform porters, parcels porters, drivers for parcels-delivery motor vans, and a batch of passenger guards. We also had a shunting yard with yard foremen and shunters working shifts. Their main work was to serve the goods department with wagons, loaded and empty, coming in and going out to meet the needs of the town. In the Mansfield area are many coal-mines, some with branch railway lines connected to the colliery sidings, so in addition to the signalboxes on the main line there were some to control the branch lines to the collieries. Part of my work consisted of visiting the outposts of my miniature empire. I needed to know what was going on and to deal with the many minor problems that continually arose. On pleasant days it was agreeable to tramp around the territory, to smell the pungent aroma of the creosoted sleepers and, where the lines passed by meadows and trees, to hear the birdsong. It was not so good in inclement weather.

At most of the places of call, I was 'sir' to the men. I didn't particularly seek this. It wasn't my style. But I think some of them either didn't know my name or couldn't pronounce it. When people were sufficiently interested to ask about its pronunciation, I explained that it rhymed with toe and not how, hoff, huff or hue.

On this kind of job, I realized the value of the training, the tedious examinations, both verbal and written, and the experience at many stations and depots that had come my way. A stationmaster, relief or otherwise, was required to know not only all the administration – from ordering passenger tickets and compiling wages bills to hiring and firing – but all the detail needed for running a goods depot. That could involve wagons of goods to whole trainloads, and all the charging processes. He also needed to know just what every man's duties were and their operating responsibilities. This embraced not only station staff but drivers and signalmen, shunters and permanent-way men. He needed to be familiar with the structure of management from top to bottom. But above all, his supreme objective, and indeed duty, was always safety.

Every two years a stationmaster was required to endure a rigorous verbal examination by a top expert from HQ, mainly on the operational side and safety. For a relief stationmaster, the pain and suffering had to be endured once every year. If you failed, you would be warned that your next chance could be your last. In that event, you could be removed from your position and offered a clerical appointment, possibly at a lower grade and a lower rate of pay. During my many years up and down the line and at HQ, I cannot recall a single instance of anyone suffering such a personal distress. That speaks well for the selection system. In such a case, HQ were fair and reasonable and would take account of individual problems such as ill health or domestic stresses.

Soon after two o'clock one afternoon, foreman Larry Clegg knocked on the door of my private office. He waited until I called, 'Come in!'

Slightly coolly I greeted him, 'Good afternoon, Foreman.'
He removed his uniform cap with a little smile. 'Good afternoon,' a little pause, then, '*sir.*'
I ignored his familiar dig and kept to business, but with a friendly demeanour. He told me, 'Porter Robson's gone to hospital for his usual monthly check. He'll be back at four. I've put Kitley on overtime to cover the gap.'
'Good!'
'Telegram here from Nottingham. They're putting a vehicle on the back of the 2.20 ex Notts with two prize bulls for Ambergate.'
'What sort of a vehicle?'
'A horsebox. Because it has partitions.'
'How does it go forward from here to Ambergate?'
'I've fixed for the goods yard foreman to pick up with an E and B.'
'Do Ambergate know it's coming?'
'Yes. I've just wired it off.'
Two bulls in one vehicle struck me as risky to say the least.
When the 2.20 p.m. arrived from Nottingham – it's just seventeen miles – I went onto the platform to keep an eye on things. Larry Clegg took charge of the detailed operations. A few passengers joined the train and a few alighted. Judging by the noises, the bulls were getting restive. A porter got down on the track and unhooked the horsebox from the back of the train, which then continued its journey of fifteen miles to Worksop.
Suddenly we heard a great bellow from one of the bulls, followed by loud banging noises, and the horsebox began to sway a little on its springs. Several passengers and few staff became rooted to where they stood, looking on somewhat startled. The little manageress of W.H. Smith's bookstall ran to the tiny cabin by the station entrance and squeezed up to a surprised ticket-collector.
The engine was now uncoupled from the goods brake van, and it backed up to the horsebox to couple up. After that, the engine and the box would back up to the van for coupling up.

Larry suddenly grabbed my arm as the banging got worse. 'Look at that, sir. One of them's goring the sides of the box. See, one horn just come through.'

'Get on the blower to the signalbox, Larry. Tell the bobby to stop all trains in both directions. Quick!'

I was about to hurry into my office to the phone when Larry questioned, 'D'you mean that, sir?'

'Of course! Don't argue, do it and bloody well quick! Then get a couple of shunters up here with shunting poles. And get a pole for me.' The poor fellow seemed in a daze. 'Hurry, man! For God's sake, move!'

From inside my office I could hear the bellowing and the banging. It was getting worse. I scanned the emergency list on my office wall. Steam-cranes, railway technical men, hospital, fire, police, doctors – everything but a vet. Ah, right at the bottom written in pencil. Mr Cyril Todd, telephone Mansfield 6995, the entry read. I was having flashes of anxious speculation. Bulls on the railway track ... terrifying passengers ... I was now dialling the number. Impatiently I began to count the ringing tones – 1, 2, 3, 4, 5 – the vet could be out or up the garden – 6, 7: 'Mansfield 6995. Todd speaking.'

'Stationmaster, Mansfield LMS, here, Mr Todd. This is urgent. We have two bulls in a railway van in the station. One is going berserk. Bellowing and crashing about. And he's damaging the vehicle.'

'Oh, I see. I'm rather busy at present ...'

'Sorry, Mr Todd. It's urgent. He's got to be stopped. Otherwise we could have a nasty accident on the line. Whatever happens, he's got to be stopped. Quickly.'

A pause. Then, 'I'm on my way.'

Back on the platform there were no passengers or anyone else to be seen. And the bellowing and banging were really frantic. A panel at the side of the horsebox now had a hole in it, and a horn kept on goring at it.

Larry arrived with two shunters, each armed with a shunting pole, and he held two, one for me. He seemed rather shaken and wide-eyed. I thought he might even be about to collapse. Breathlessly, he asked, 'Anybody come yet, Guv?'

'The vet's on his way. Should be here any minute.'

We took up our positions on the platform near the vehicle, which was now rocking dangerously on its springs. Feeling pretty helpless, we stood there as the noise and damage to the vehicle grew worse.

Hearing the squeal of car brakes, I hurried to the station entrance. Mr Todd, fortyish, in rough tweeds and with two bags, a short one and a long one, remarked, 'Yes, I can hear the blighter. Making quite a fuss, isn't he!'

As we walked briskly along the platform, the vet seemed remarkably cool and relaxed. What was a lifetime's experience for me was no doubt routine for him. We stood on the platform alongside the horsebox, and judging by his antics the bull was obviously working up to a climax.

'If I can get near enough,' explained the vet, 'I'll try him with a strong sedative. I say, that's a large gap on the side there. If he gets his shoulder or his haunches in view, I might be able to give him the works.'

For minutes he tried to use his large syringe, but without result, and the bull was becoming ever more frantic. From his long bag, the vet produced a stubby sort of rifle, placed a bullet into the breech, then took his time to get the animal's forehead into his sights. It was a breathless moment. In the middle of a mighty bellow, the bull must have charged his head at the hole at the side. Mr Todd was poised ready. Then, 'Bang!' Just for a few seconds, the bellowing changed to moaning, then silence. We heard a heavy thud, telling us that the animal had fallen to the floor of the vehicle. The peak of danger was now over.

Almost as an afterthought, I told the vet, 'They are both prize bulls.'

'It would have made no difference, Stationmaster. He was very soon going to get himself out of that vehicle. And then we would have had real trouble.'

I called to the guard of the engine, horsebox and brake van. 'I want to get this lot off the main line. Draw forward into number one siding, George, and I'll come along to see what the next move is.'

That enabled us to declare the lines in both directions clear of obstruction, and I reported details to Nottingham control office. They had already heard of the hold-up earlier from my signalman.

Mr Todd and I walked along to number one siding, and the vet examined the second bull, a smaller animal and quite docile. 'Maybe,' said the vet, 'he is already sedated. They both should have been for a journey like this one.'

Most competently the vet took everything in hand. He arranged with the local abattoir to cope with the dead bull's carcass and for a local farmer to tend the other bull until the owners could be contacted. He promised to send me a report on the whole episode, together with his account, which I undertook to forward to Derby HQ.

From the waybill for the bulls' journey, and the label on the side of the horsebox, I obtained the sender's name and address. I sent a telegram to him, and a copy to the stationmaster at Bedford, the sending station. For quite a time afterwards it was the talk of the district. On several occasions I was to hear the story second or third hand; bits of it matched the facts of the case, almost.

Meantime, many tricky questions remained unanswered. Somebody would have to explain whether the offending bull had been properly prepared for the journey, short though it was, and why both bulls had been loaded into the one vehicle. Compensation for the loss of the bull would have to be faced. So too would be the costs of repairing the damaged railway vehicle. But how could I give a damn? They were questions for my HQ masters to grapple with, enough to keep them busy for months. I had plenty on my plate to keep my station working safely.

Apart from the load of bull, the fortnight as stationmaster was passing pleasantly enough. Being at Mansfield offered the bonus of having the midday meal with my wife and small son, our home being only ten minutes away on foot and five minutes by bike.

From time to time there was a little light relief at the station. For example, at 3.10 p.m. precisely I visited the ladies' toilet. Mid afternoon was a quiet period between trains, and it was also convenient for station foreman Larry

Clegg to come with me. I carried a small book bearing the title, 'Lav Cash Book', plus the keys to the penny-in-the slot doors. According to the standard cash regulations, the lavatory-emptying job was a two-man task. You see, it was all loose and spendable cash. When those mysterious assemblers of the cash regulations at HQ compiled their deathless prose, they took serious account of human nature. One man alone emptying the cash locks might be tempted to do a little fiddle on the side. But whatever anyone said about the LMS accounting systems, they were virtually fiddle-proof. To pull off a really successful fiddle with the Lav Cash, you would require the loyal services of a totally trustworthy fellow felon. And by the time you had worked out a foolproof fiddling system, along would come that totally untrustworthy fellow the travelling auditor, right in the middle of your fancy felony, and botch the whole thing up. Besides, there were too many foreign coins and metal washers to finance a trip to Southend, never mind South America, even if you lived long enough.

In the summer I was back at Mansfield for a few days in place of the junior clerk in the booking-office who was on leave. I was working the early shift, 5 a.m. to 2 p.m., the same as Larry Clegg. Since the episode with the bull, he had been a little subdued in my company, but this morning he couldn't help ragging me. 'Come on now, me lad. Get on with it!'

'Certainly, sir,' I responded. 'Three bags full, sir!'

The passengers I booked up to eight o'clock usually wanted workmen's daily return tickets, which were very cheap. A young man who didn't look much like the usual workman type, carrying a suitcase, came to the window.

'I have a ticket already from Nottingham to London,' he explained. 'So I'll take a single ticket to Nottingham, please.'

'Why not take a workman's ticket? It's a lot cheaper.'

'I shan't be coming back. A single will do fine.'

'A single ticket is 2s.9d. A workman's ticket is only 1s.2d. If you have a workman's, it'll save you 1s.7d. What d'you think, sir?'

'Yes, I see exactly what you mean. But I'd better take the ordinary single.'

So I made 1s.7d. more profit for the LMS Railway Company's shareholders. I wonder how much they would care for my efforts on their behalf?

Most passengers would have bought the cheaper ticket. Besides, offering a choice followed my usual practice of always helping the passenger to get the cheapest ticket available for his particular journey. I claim no credit for this. After all, it cost me nothing. I was only giving the railway company's money away.

12
Enough to Give You the Creeps

The scene now shifts to another time and place, near Birmingham.

'We've got to get rid of that there creep,' the permanent-way ganger told me on the track. But before we get rid of that creep, a comment. His remark reminded me that one of the most fascinating features about a job on the railways was the astonishing variety of work that has to be done to keep the steam trains running. Every trade and calling you can think of is involved, from artisans to the professions. In addition to the station staff whom we know so well, there are painters and decorators, joiners and stonemasons, bricklayers and glaziers, mechanics and motor drivers, professional engineers (locomotive, civil, electrical, signalling and telecommunications, motor, maritime), architects, veterinary surgeons, doctors, solicitors, barristers, tutors, writers, police. And a few more besides.

I have always been intrigued by the other man's job. While acting as stationmaster at Wylde Green, a suburban station roughly half way between Birmingham and Lichfield, you can imagine my interest at seeing a gang of workers get off a train and descend upon the track. Like Snow White's seven dwarfs, they carried on their shoulders picks and shovels, keying and sledgehammers and other tools. I half expected them to break into melodious song, in Walt Disney style, 'Hey ho, hey ho, and off to work we go, hey ho.' You can visualize passengers gazing through the windows of passing trains and wondering what the men were up to, apparently doing nothing but lean on their shovels. Which gives me the chance to dispose of a railway track-side myth. Men working on the track are exposed to great danger. While the trains are passing, they need to stand still on most occasions for their personal safety. And for their protection, a look-out man stands by the track. He wears a red armlet lettered 'Look-out' and carries a horn to sound a warning note, rather like John Peel's hunting-horn.

Hoping to see someone in authority, I walked along the track. A few days ago, I recalled, a permanent-way inspector had inspected this section of the line, and I assumed that the work in hand must have resulted from his findings. Some years back I had joined the Permanent Way Institution as a student member. We visited steelworks where rails were made, unique track layouts like the famous diamond crossing at Newcastle-upon-Tyne, the high-speed track near Peterborough, and the station layouts at Edinburgh Waverley and St Enoch's, Glasgow. During the process I had acquired a modicum of knowledge about railway tracks, at least to be able to say 'yes' and 'no' in the right places.

This particular morning at Wylde Green, along the line I came across the ganger-in-charge and greeted him, 'A nice day for your job, Ganger.'

'You be right, sir. But my weathercock say this morning there be rain to come afore teatime. Today we be a-gettin' rid of that theer creep. It's getting bad again.'

I had been watching the men knock out wooden keys from the iron chairs in which the rails sat, the chairs in turn resting on the wooden sleepers that lay on the track bed of ballast. I also saw them moving the rails. But for the life of me, I just couldn't fathom what they were up to.

'Tell me, Ganger. What's the routine?'

He knocked the ash out of his clay pipe by tapping it gently on his heel, and he loosened his red spotted neckerchief as the morning sun was warming up. 'You slacks off them keys and the fishplates, and you moves the rails backards or forrards. And you watch for cracks in them fishplates.'

'Oh, I see.' I didn't really see at all, but you can't tell a bloke that, can you? I tried hard to look intelligent.

He continued, 'If the line's downhill, you pulls them rails back a bit. And if it's uphill, you pushes the rails forrards a bit.'

'Yes, I see.' I didn't let on that I was seeing it clearly for the first time. But I got the point, and thought – how simple. Like all great ideas when you come to think about them, just simple.

The rails were made in lengths of sixty feet. Between the ends of the rails a small space or gap was left, about half an inch or more. This was to allow for expansion in the intense heat of summer, and contraction in intense cold in winter. In time the gaps are slightly increased or decreased with the continuous pounding from heavy trains. Without the gap at the end of the rails, the track could become buckled during very high temperatures in the summer. And when the track buckles, the trains come off the rails – which, thankfully, is rather rare.

On a rising gradient, the grip of the driving wheels tends to drag the rails to the rear. Only fractionally, mind you. Hardly measurable. After many months, or even years, the gaps between the ends of the rails on a rising gradient tend to get smaller, and on a falling gradient they tend to get wider. Going on a falling gradient, downhill, the engine often does not have to pull. It 'freewheels'. On a falling gradient, the driver often has to apply his brakes, and the drag of the wheels tends to push the rails forward, also only a tiny fraction, and gaps between the ends of the rails become wider. These very slight movements of the rails, backwards or forwards, are known, it appears, as 'rail creep'.

Those gaps at the ends of the rails render the rhythm, well known on a railway journey, that sounds something like this: diddle-ee-dee diddle-ee-dah, diddle-ee-dee diddle-ee-dah. It is the knowledge of these rail-end joints that can give you the edge on your fellow travellers. This should enable you to accost one of them with the supreme confidence of expert knowledge.

For example, on an express one day, the gentleman sitting opposite was obviously interested in my stopwatch, pencil and notebook. He grinned and said, 'What are you up to?'

'I'm checking the speed of the train.'

He leaned forward. 'How d'you do it?'

'I count the number of the joints in the rails for forty-one seconds, and that gives the miles per hour.'

'Oh, most interesting. What are we doing now?'

'About seventy, I'd think.'

He seemed thoughtful. 'But why forty-one?'

'A railway engineer told me some years ago. He said they'd worked it out in the office.'

If the train happens to be travelling on a main-line stretch of the new long-welded track, you can't really count the joints. The rail ends are welded solid for a smoother ride. Long-welded is different from the older and much more widely used type known as bull-head rail. Partly because of its broader base, the flat-bottomed type is able to absorb more effectively the expansion and contraction of the rails caused by changes of temperature in the extremes of summer and winter. I don't have to be a magician or consult my crystal ball to forecast that this flat-bottom track is very superior and has a great future.

Let us now get back to Wylde Green.

In the afternoon it began to rain. The ganger had had an accurate forecast from his weathercock, which, I presume, was a fir cone and had closed in anticipation of rain. From the station platform, I could see the gang of men packing up their tools, and they ambled along the platform to catch the 3.55 p.m. train to Birmingham. As the ganger climbed aboard with his men, he shouted to me, 'Us'll be back tomorrer, sir, to finish off that bloody creep.'

I was glad that no innocent passenger was near. He might have misinterpreted an innocuous remark and just wouldn't know how to put it to his folks when he got back home.

It is sad to think that this new-fangled flat-bottom rail will eventually banish for ever the term 'rail creep' from railway permanent-way jargon. And, sadder still for some people, 'diddle-ee-dah'.

The scene changes. I am now busy booking tickets in Derby booking-office. One of the other two clerks, Ian Macgregor, created for himself an awkward situation, and he was embarrassed as he tried to extricate himself. Behind the scenes it was comic.

He wore his old bottle-green office jacket, with brown leather patches at the elbows, making his short stature look even shorter. Aged forty, he had left his native Scotland while in his early teens and nursed his rugged Glasgow accent proudly, even when nobody could understand a word he said. When we discovered that the braces which held up his trousers were in a brilliant tartan, he rolled up a trouser-leg to show that he had suspenders to match, the suspenders holding up his tartan socks.

'Dinna ye laugh at them, mon. Or ye'll have the entire mad Clan Macgregor rise up in their graves in the Highlands and haunt ye for everrmorre!'

In a happy mood, he would sing a Harry Lauder comic song, such as, 'I belong to Glasgow', with commendable mimicry. But today his mood was far from happy. His books just would not balance after a heavy session of ticket booking. And they simply must balance to a halfpenny for the chief clerk's full daily balance.

At the slide-door of his booking window for London came a gentle tap. He ignored it. Then two taps. He muttered something Gaelic under his breath. A pause. Then still more taps. He suddenly flung his slide-door up and bawled fiercely, 'No trrain due yet. I'm open in half an hourr, madam.' He banged the door down savagely, distracting my own figurework. Before it closed, I just managed to get a glimpse of the passenger, a little old lady.

Some minutes later came another knock – firm, decisive. Ian slid up his little door and, without looking to see who was there, bellowed in his rich and rugged Scottish, 'There's no trrain yet. I'm open in twenty minutes.' He banged his slide-door down again. Then he addressed the office in general, in a forthright tone, 'D'ye know, chaps, I hate the bloody passengers. They spoil the job forr me!'

Poor Ian. He was breathing heavily now, and his face was flushed. He was struggling against the clock with his bookwork. He knew that the chief clerk would come to him shortly to collect his cash takings for banking.

Immediately came a more determined knocking. Furiously he slid up his door and I heard a man's voice say firmly, 'Single to London, please.'

With a sigh, Ian began his explanation once more. 'No trrain to London for overr half an hourr yet. Come back in fifteen minutes.'

He was about to close his window when the man persisted.

'Look here, you're the booking-clerk. I'm the customer. I want a single ticket to London. Now, please. It's for my elderly mother. You refused her some minutes ago, but I won't allow you to refuse me.'

His voice was quiet but commanding. But Ian was still stubborn.

'I tell ye, there's no trrain yet. I'll open up in good time.'

The passenger's tone rose half a decibel. 'I want that ticket this moment. My mother's travelling tomorrow and I'm sending her luggage in advance today. Your luggage people require to see the travel ticket first, and to endorse it. My next move will be to see the stationmaster.'

Poor old Ian. He'd met his match. Deflated and subdued, he issued the ticket to London with a gruff semi-apology and continued to mutter Gaelic oaths under his breath. I was so embarrassed for him that I kept my eyes glued to my paperwork. The other clerk had been too busy on his Manchester window to take much notice.

I understood how he felt, up to a point. Booking tickets at a large station, including all the related daily, weekly and monthly accounting and statistical tasks, could be a job of real pressure. Especially in the busy summer months. For any length of time, I would have hated it. But I never hated the passengers. On the contrary ...

13
Pulling the Elephant's Leg

If you find this incident hard to believe, I found it harder. It just goes to show how fancy schemes can have their perfidious flaws.

When I went to Teversall for one day while the regular stationmaster, Roger Bowman, visited London HQ, the young clerk told me the trip was to collect his 'Quota Shield'.

This Quota Shield business had been introduced in the 1930s by the chief commercial superintendent of the LMS Railway, a dynamic character with drive and energy named Ashton Davies. Trained on the former Lancashire & Yorkshire Railway, he rose to become a vice-president of the LMS under the great Sir Josiah (later Lord) Stamp. The aim of the Quota was to encourage stationmasters and their staff to canvass vigorously for new business, for both passengers and parcels traffic. At HQ in London, a quota of average takings was recorded for each station throughout the LMS system. Shields were awarded to those stationmasters who had secured the best increases, area by area, in one year. Increases based on percentages placed large and small stations on the same footing. A monthly staff newspaper called *Quota News* described how the system worked, encouraged the staff to use their initiative and publicized the lucky winners.

Late in the afternoon, Mr Bowman returned with his shining prize, an area Quota Shield. It was lettered with basic details, the name 'Teversall' having been engraved in an oblong panel. It was mounted on a piece of polished light oak which had a splendid grain.

Since Teversall was now only a goods and minerals station, passenger trains having long been withdrawn, I asked: 'Tell me, Roger Bowman. How can a small goods station with no passenger trains win a shield for the passenger business?'

I sat at his big old desk in one of the most untidy goods offices in Nottinghamshire. His countryman's face, round and ruddy and adorned by a fair moustache and with hair to match, creased jovially and the mention of the shield made him explode with bubbling laughter.

Recovering, he said, 'It's a cockeyed situation. Occasionally a Teversall family will come here for holiday tickets. They travel from Mansfield but, as you know, they have to pay for their passenger tickets in advance. Then I can send our motor van to pick up their luggage to send in advance of their journey.'

'I presume you have the luggage sent on a passenger train from Mansfield.'

'Right. And because we don't have any passenger tickets in stock here, I write out tickets for their journey on an excess fare receipt. All I do is phone Mansfield to find out how much, then I take their money, which I enter in my books.'

Mansfield is only a few miles distant by road. So, still not comprehending, I asked him, 'But how did you come to win the shield? How did you increase your takings for passengers?'

'Simple,' he grinned. 'Last year I booked only one family to Scarborough. But this year I booked two families to the same place. So my takings for passenger tickets jumped a hundred per cent!'

His merriment brought tears to his eyes and I found his hilarity infectious.

'That's marvellous, Roger!'

'You imagine. Even Euston couldn't do that. Nor Leicester. Nor Manchester or Liverpool.'

'Couldn't do what?'

'Double their takings, man!'

'And you went all the way to London just for that shield?'

'Sure I did. In my Sunday suit. And it was handed to me personally by the great Mr Ashton Davies himself. With his congratulations to me personally, you understand?'

'You're giving me the giggles, Roger.'

'It was a big gathering. In the shareholders' meeting-room. Marvellous do. They gave us sherry. But I'd have preferred a pint o' best bitter. Ashton Davies said to me, "I see you've doubled your takings in just one year. You and your staff must have worked very hard indeed. I see you were competing in your area against Nottingham and Derby, Chesterfield and Sheffield. Well done!" ' Roger broke off for a noisy guffaw. 'My staff. Look, he's there. That right, George? When Ashton was saying all these nice things, I could hardly keep a straight face, especially after that sherry. Some of the other stationmasters know all about Teversall, and they didn't half pull my leg.'

'It's one of those freak anomalies, I suppose.'

He gave the shield an extra polish, held it up to the light to admire it and placed it on the office mantelshelf. There it vibrated visibly as a long coal train, hauled by a powerful class-four goods steam-engine, roared and clattered through the station.

'Well,' he remarked with a chuckle. 'Nice story to tell my friends!'

'And your grandchildren.'

On another visit to Teversall two months later, I came across a copy of the latest *Quota News* in Roger's top drawer. On the picture page, there was Roger Bowman, grinning widely, shaking hands and accepting the coveted escutcheon from Mr Ashton Davies. The caption under the photograph read, 'Another proud Quota Shield Winner – Doubled his takings in a year ...'

It so happened that, during the morning, I had received through the post a printed circular letter from the chief auditor in London. It demanded imperiously, 'This is the third application for your collected passenger tickets for week ending the 5th instant. Please despatch them immediately by first train.'

A cheeky impulse prompted me to reply, in bold red ink across the face of the letter, which I returned by post, 'Alas, sir, no passenger trains have run on this line since you were in your playpen.'

I heard no more. I had hoped to receive a follow-up letter enquiring how we had won the Quota Shield for passenger business without any passenger trains, but I was denied that pleasure.

Dr Richard Beeching, Railways Board Chairman, in jovial mood, amusing railway enthusiasts sampling the famous Bluebell Line.

The author at lunch in the 'Junior Officers' Mess', Marylebone. With him are Julian Harris, a PR man, Keith Horrox, editor of *Railnews,* and Bill Newton, an advertising executive.

This magnificent building – from 1948 BR HQ and lovingly known as the 'Kremlin' – began life as the Great Central Hotel, terminus of the new GCR which opened in 1899.

Left: Viscount Churchill, GWR Chairman 1908–34 – one of the greatest of the 20th-century chairmen, and a man Frank Ferneyhough has long admired. Right: Alan Pegler, the most popular railway enthusiast in Britain, here acting as courier on the famous Venice Simplon-Orient-Express.

Holiday time at Arley on the Severn Valley private railway linking Bridgnorth and Kidderminster.

Two most famous LNER locomotives: *Sir Nigel Gresley*, named after its designer, and *Flying Scotsman* no. 4472, with which Alan Pegler toured America in 1969.

Butler-Henderson, one of the many 4-4-0 express types named after GCR directors, was built in 1920.

Top: *Henry Oakley*, built at Doncaster in 1898, served on the
LNER until 1937. It was the first Atlantic type 4-4-2 in Britain.

Above: Another famous Doncaster locomotive, *Blue Peter*. Built
in 1948 for the strenuous Edinburgh – Aberdeen route, it
'retired' in 1966 and was adopted by the BBC television programme of the same name.

Two very long coal trains of the early 1940s, from the
mines at Taff Vale. Note the line-side allotments, part of the
wartime 'grow more food' campaign.

MIXED TRAFFIC STEAM LOCOMOTIVE
B·R. STANDARD DESIGN—CLASS 7.

KEY

1 FIREBOX	9 COUPLING RODS
2 BOILER-TUBES	10 SMOKE-DEFLECTORS
3 SMOKEBOX	11 SAFETY VALVE
4 STEAM CHEST	12 INJECTORS
5 VALVE GEAR	13 SANDING PIPES
6 CYLINDER	14 SUPERHEATING TUBES
7 PISTON	
8 CONNECTING ROD	

Inside the complicated works of a class 7 BR standard class 4-6-2 Pacific type for working both fast passenger and fast freight trains.

An old print of Shrewsbury station standing in the shadow of the castle. This handsome structure is the work of the architect T.M. Penson and is still today a joy to the eye.

Slip-coaches, last operated in 1960. The rear guard disconnects the two rear coaches and brings them to a standstill while the express continues on its way.

Yet another idea for the channel tunnel that came to naught!

Throughout their history, the railways have shown their ingenuity in a million ways. This rail-mounted device made the vital inspection of bridges always quick and easy.

As a relief man, I covered a fairly wide area and often, when returning to a station where I had been in charge before, I was conscious of hoping for a reasonable welcome on each succeeding visit. Of course, you could be greeted in quite a warm way. But a man could be muttering to a colleague – Oh, not that bastard again, or that bighead, or that creep, or that stickler for the rules, or that chap who always comes late and goes home early. Thankfully, I was never to know.

When you revisit a station, you soon become aware whether you are liked or disliked. Much depended on the style of the regular stationmaster. I have sometimes been talked into taking some action which, according to the staff, the stationmaster kept on dodging. But you never knew for sure. If the regular gaffer was a crusty old gent approaching retirement, your welcome was assured. But if he was weak and ineffective and the staff pleased themselves, you had a problem.

Anyway, I was sent to Stanton Gate on the Erewash Valley main line between Nottingham and Chesterfield for two weeks. There were four lines of track, and it was a busy route. Express passenger trains, long coal trains and trains of empty wagons roared and steamed up and down the line day and night. At Stanton Gate was a marshalling yard. It was open twenty-four hours a day and was manned by shunters doing shift work.

A note had been left for me by the regular stationmaster that shunter Noles had been absent on the sicklist for Friday and Saturday and that he would resume duty on the night shift starting at ten o'clock on the Monday night. On the Tuesday morning I learnt that Noles had not turned up for work. The afternoon man, instead of finishing at 10 p.m., had to stay on until 2 a.m., and the man who would normally have come on at six in the morning had to be sent for from home to start at 2 a.m. Their wives would not be very pleased.

One of the clerks said in confidence, 'Noles is a damn' nuisance. He's not a long-serving railwayman. He was appointed during the war, and in peace-time he's still a nuisance. Comes and goes when he likes and messes his mates up no end.'

'Why doesn't the stationmaster sack him?'

'He doesn't want the trouble. I don't want to talk behind his back. He's a good sort, but he's too nice for some people. They take advantage of him.'

'Thanks for telling me. I appreciate it.'

He turned as he went to the door. 'There's another thing. I'm told Noles is moonlighting in something or other. I think he just uses the railway for his own purposes.'

'Leave it with me, Mr Blake.'

I hadn't met Mr Blake before. He seemed a reliable chap. In his forties. Was he being truthful? He sounded convincing but I had to be sure. I made one or two soundings that finally satisfied me.

On the Tuesday afternoon I received a phone call, obviously from a post-office telephone call-box. 'Hallo, sir. Shunter Noles a-talkin'. I be coming back to work tonight, sir. Ten o'clock.'

'Have you a medical certificate, Noles?'

'No, sir. Don't want none. I'm back at work tonight, see?'

I reminded him of the regulations. 'You've been away three days, and a medical certificate is needed. You understand?'

'Yessir. But I just said. I be a-comin' back to work tonight, you see.'

I decided to give him the rough treatment. 'You're wasting your time and money on this call. Good day.'

'Eh, who be that a-talkin'?'

'The relief stationmaster. You've just said you'll be at work tonight. But you said that you'd be back at work last night, and you didn't turn up. We had to get your two mates to cover your turn of duty.'

'But I'm better now, sir.'

'You broke your word last night. Why should I believe you now?'

'What's me orders then, sir?'

'I can't give you any because I can't depend on you. We can't run a railway like this.'

'What shall I do, then?'

'Stay at home. We'll send for you when we want you. If we

want you. Good day!' I hung up.

We were still under a government order concerning the control of employment. It was an emergency regulation from the recent war and still in force. So you couldn't sack a man just like that, whatever he'd done, almost. But I was determined to shift this blighter.

I telephoned the district officer at Nottingham, explained the background and emphasized that it was far from an isolated case; he gave me permission to go through the motions and to sack the man. I obtained the appropriate form from the local employment office, sent it to Nottingham to be countersigned, then posted it to Noles, and that was that. Afterwards, several of the staff came up to me and said nice things. This came as a surprise but was a welcome bonus.

The next time I went to Stanton Gate, I learnt that Noles had been doing decorating work. This fitted in with his railway shifts, but his interest in the LMS Railway was nil. It was never easy to sack a man on the railway, unless he had done something really outrageous. In my entire career, Noles was the only fellow I ever dismissed from the railway. Mind you, I nearly had the sack myself once or twice. Maybe I was lucky.

Mr Pompson was an awkward cuss. I was at his station for two days to make an independent check on his customer accounts that had still not been paid. It was a regular and routine task. I asked to see his station account books. At once he put on his awkward squad act. 'I'm going to the signalbox awhile. It can wait until I come back.' He made for the door.

'But I only want ...' And he was gone.

As a stationmaster, he was not known for tact and diplomacy. Passengers sometimes complained. Nothing serious. Just irritating. I thought – damn you, Mr Pompson, I want to get on with my work. So I rummaged through his drawers and cupboards, hoping to find the authorized accounts. But he must have kept them under lock and key. Having no luck, I put the kettle on the gas-ring in the office and made a cup of coffee. Then I picked up the stationmaster's *Daily Mirror*, read the news in five minutes and dallied with the strip cartoons. One featured that tantalizing blonde called Jane, tailed by her faithful hound, Fritz. As usual, our heroine was about to lose her frilly panties. Another concerned that dastardly villain Captain Jasper Reilly-Ffoul, who was just calling in his bailiff to sell off the home of an innocent damsel who refused to bend to his will.

I was chuckling at these antics when in strode Mr Pompson, scowling fiercely. He grabbed the paper from my hand. 'That's mine when you've done with it. I've just had a bloody row with my signalman and I'm ready for another if you are!'

What a nice man. He had the sallow, lined face of one who has worked shifts for many years, and the self-importance of a man thrown into authority but not born to be a master of his fellows.

Like a goodly proportion of his kind, he had started life as a junior porter at fifteen, found he had a knack for learning the operating rules, was a porter-signalman at twenty-two and a full signalman three years later. Having been noticed by a visiting head office inspector from Derby as worthy of promotion, he was given training in his off-duty time, at the station where he worked, under the guidance of the stationmaster. This was fairly common at one period. But Mr Pompson was no great shakes with the paperwork. On two occasions in the past, I had been sent there to lend a hand for a few hours with his timebook and wages bill. On both occasions I had felt he qualified principally as a high-ranking member of the awkward squad. I learnt that his father had been a farm labourer who looked after the pigs and was naturally mighty proud of his son for rising up in the world. His kind, thankfully not very numerous, chucked their weight around and tended to use bullying tactics with their few staff rather than gentle persuasion.

His first station was a tiny wayside affair that you might easily have carried away on the back of a lorry if nobody was looking. His total staff consisted of one porter and one level-crossing keeper. Some years later he had a slightly larger station, and in due course his present station, which was graded three and where I was engaged in checking his unpaid accounts. Now nearly fifty, with about a dozen staff, he needed a larger size in gold-braid caps. His style reminded me of lines from Shakespeare's *Measure for Measure*: 'But man, proud man, dressed in a little brief authority. Most ignorant of what he is most assured.'

Though he fancied he knew the operating rules backwards, he often broke them to suit himself. I was to learn later that in the signalbox he finally had his comeuppance. The signalman was about to authorize an engine and brake van to move into the section ahead, then to return on the same line. For the return run, the driver would need to proceed 'in the wrong direction', for which a special form, called a 'wrong line order', was required. He was about to fill in the form when the stationmaster intervened.

'You don't need that, man,' he grunted. 'It's a waste of time. Dammit, it's broad daylight and clear weather!'

'I think we does, sir.' His tone was respectful.

The goods guard off the brake van had come into the box to see about the 'wrong line order'. In an inferior's presence, the stationmaster could not have one of his signalmen telling him what could and could not be done, so he barked, 'I say we don't need no WLO and that's that!'

Previously the signalman had suffered similar exchanges. This time he stood his ground. 'We'll be breaking the rules, Mr Pompson.'

Angrily the stationmaster shouted. 'And I say we won't have a WLO. And that's final!'

'If you says so.'

The guard was acutely embarrassed, for he too would know that the WLO form was needed for the operation, and off he went.

A month or so later the stationmaster was removed from his grade three position and, in a disciplinary process, transferred to a smaller station elsewhere, graded four and with a drop in salary. The signalman, who had suffered enough, had reported the irregularity to Derby HQ. He was able to do so, however, only because the goods guard with him in the box at the time had undertaken to be a witness.

I was sorry for the fellow really, for he was his own worst enemy. The station to which he had been transferred was outside my territory and I never came across him again, which brought me no grief at all.

At Sutton-in-Ashfield, near Mansfield, we had a circus elephant to send away by train to Cardiff. Stubborn as a mule? We had to get a steam-engine to move this one. He had been entertaining the children of miners at Sutton. Now it was time for him to go on his travels again to audiences new. His name was Eli.

Two days earlier I had ordered from central rolling-stock control at Derby the large van in which the animal would travel. It was scheduled to be loaded at 8 a.m. and to depart attached to the rear of a train due to leave at 8.30 a.m. Knowing not a thing about the travel habits of circus elephants, I was naturally the man for the job.

That morning I took my small son to watch the fun, if any. The van stood in the dock, which was a short platform connected to the running lines. Its end doors were already open. At eight o'clock precisely I saw a large grey elephant, its enormous ears flapping, being led along Station Road by an Indian. The Indian was slight of build and wore a fawn, smock-like garment, yellow, well-worn sandals and a white turban with a red strip across the forehead.

Greeting him, I asked his name. I wanted my son to hear this foreign gentleman speak. We had no Indians living in Mansfield. The man said, in pure cockney, 'Me name's Dick Johnson.' Surprise, surprise. I had expected something like 'Mahatma Pundit Patel'.

He led Eli towards the empty van, but the elephant resisted. He must have weighed at least a couple of tons. Two tons of stubborn resistance against a man of slight build spelled for me delay to the 8.30 a.m. when it came in. The elephant slipped into reverse gear against the pressure of the handler's viciously pointed iron implement, a necessary tool against one with so thick a skin.

Suddenly he threw up his trunk and let out a tremendous

trumpeting which made my little lad hide behind me in fright. It was beginning to look rather ugly. I just didn't feel quite at home with elephants. I had already telegraphed ahead to inform station junctions where the van would have to be shunted from one train to another, and to Cardiff, the destination station. I had also compiled a waybill with charges for the elephant's journey.

Again the handler tried to persuade the huge, grey, crinkle-skinned monster towards the van, but still no joy. Nearby was a small tank-engine with six coupled wheels shunting and steaming up and down the sidings, placing wagons into position. It was then that an idea struck me. I calculated that steam-engine pulling-power exceeded elephant resistance-power by a goodly margin. Leaving my son at a safe distance and telling him not to move, I walked across to the shunting engine to sound the driver about my idea.

'Seems all right to me, boss. We'll have a go.'

Back I went and explained to the handler. He too was agreeable. From the goods warehouse I took a coil of wire hauser. The driver of the shunting engine moved to a position close by the van. We secured one end of the hauser to the engine and passed the other end through the open doors of the van into which we hoped to persuade Eli to enter, and out through the opening at the other end. Finally the handler secured the hauser to the elephant's right front leg where his ankle ought to be.

Hopefully I signalled to the engine-driver to move very gently until the hauser was taut. The slight pull on the leg made the elephant ease forward his other three legs by a few inches. The driver kept up a gentle pressure with the hauser, without making too much upsetting noise with his exhaust steam. We didn't want a frightened elephant running amok in the goods yard. I wouldn't know where to look in our Rule Book as to what action to take. There might not be a rule to tell me. I don't think there's anything in it about elephants.

And so it went on, little by little, until we had Eli safely and surely inside the van, and the handler secured him with ropes to the iron rings in the van. There was little chance of his being thrown about during the journey, for he practically filled the van, his head almost reaching the roof.

When he was settled, he began to sway gently from his front right leg to his rear left leg in a simple rhythm, swinging his trunk in unison with an accompanying squeak from the springs of the van. Slapping his hand on the elephant's crinkly buttocks, Dick Johnson, the Indian, much relieved, grinned. 'Eli's happy now. That's just what he does in the circus ring when the band begins to play.'

With its circus cargo, the passenger train departed exactly at half past eight. My small son had enjoyed watching an elephant having its leg pulled.

14

Why Are We Going Backwards, Guard?

Working as a peripatetic, a fortnight here, two days there, here today and gone tomorrow, sometimes as a stationmaster, sometimes as a chief clerk or a junior, one thing was essential: I had to work within the official Rule Book. I must never be persuaded into taking unnecessary risks.

I ran into a knavish situation while working as yardmaster at Hasland, a marshalling yard serving a group of collieries just south of Chesterfield on the main line to Nottingham. In a recent mishap, two empty wagons had been derailed on the up slow line and had toppled down a steep embankment. Arrangements were made for them to be lifted back onto the track by steam crane one Sunday. On that occasion it came through to me loud and clear, not for the first time, how easily a small error of judgement might cause an express train crash.

Alongside the up slow line, where the two wagons had been derailed, ran the down slow. Next came the up fast line and the down fast. Altogether, four lines of way. My responsibility would be for the operating safety of the entire movements. The locomotive inspector, Mr Bernard Barlowe, from Hasland engine sheds, would supervise the working of the steam crane.

To reach the scene of the mishap, on the Sunday morning, our short train left the engine sheds about nine o'clock. It consisted of an 0-6-0 steam-engine, a wagon loaded with timbers and packing, a wagon to take the overhang of the jib of the crane, the steam-crane already in steam, an empty wagon and a goods brake van.

I rode in the van with the guard, three cranemen and the locomotive-inspector. We chugged away gently for almost a mile to reach the signalbox on the up side. There the inspector and I explained to the signalman just what we were going to do.

I hadn't met Mr Barlowe, the inspector, before. His was a salaried supervisory post two grades higher than mine; he was my senior, in fact, and much more experienced. I thought he must be in his mid-fifties. I wore my usual uniform, including a gold-braided cap lettered 'Stationmaster'. He wore a navy-blue uniform suit and the ubiquitous bowler hat.

The move we planned was to run our steam-crane train forward into the section ahead for about a mile, set up the crane to rescue the two derailed wagons, which might take two or three hours, then return in the reverse direction to where we had started, at the signalbox and into the sidings. The signalman at the other end of the section would be told on the internal telephone, and telegraphic signals exchanged.

Running a train in the reverse direction against the flow of other trains, especially on a main line, if not done correctly can obviously be a dangerous operation. That part was *my* baby, and mine alone.

The official rules set out exactly what had to be done and by whom. A special 'wrong line order' (WLO) form had to be issued by the signalman and countersigned by me. Details had to be entered by the signalman in his train register book, and the form handed to the driver of the train as his authority to return to the signalbox in the wrong direction when the job was done.

In the signalbox, I was discussing these details. Then Inspector Barlowe, who seemed in a testy and aggressive mood, barked, 'To blazes with wrong line orders. Let's get on with the bloody job and home to Sunday dinner.'

The signalman shot an anxious glance at me. If he failed to issue the prescribed form, he would be breaking an important rule, but if the inspector and I agreed to do it that way, the signalman would have little option but to accept our authority.

In my mind, there was absolutely no doubt. I told the inspector, 'We'll have to do the job properly ...'

He barged in roughly, 'Oh my God, another rules man,

eh? Stick to the rules and stop the job, eh? Don't you want to get back for your dinner?'

His tone was scornful. Not much use arguing with a man like this. I said, quietly but firmly, 'Signalman, OK for the form now, please.'

Swearing loudly, Mr Barlowe stamped out of the signalbox and clattered down the steps to the track, and climbed into the brake van. I went down to the track and handed the WLO form to the driver. I then climbed into the brake van, told the guard about the WLO form and asked him to signal to the driver to start.

In the van an ugly silence reigned as we steamed along the line for about a mile to the site of the derailed wagons. Ordinarily the conversation would have been lively and friendly, and we would all have been in a happy mood. I was sorry that the inspector and I had clashed. We each shouldered personal responsibility in our respective spheres, and it wasn't good for men in charge to be in an ugly mood. I didn't like it. It is disorientating to the clear thinking processes.

However, there we were in the morning sunshine at this lonely spot, railway metals shining brightly, fresh green fields and trees for miles around, and here and there birdsong from thrush and blackbird. Everybody got busy with allotted tasks of rescuing the two derailed wagons, each weighing about six tons. The steam-crane was chugging away with the crane driver at the controls, and the jib stretching over the embankment.

Not altogether trusting Inspector Barlowe, I kept alert. I had already seen that the wheels of the steam-crane vehicle were firmly fixed to the rails, gripped by its special clamps, as prescribed in the operating rules. One rescued wagon was now high on the jib of the crane, but the jib couldn't be swung round because the railway telegraph wires on the track side were in the way. This would entail putting the wagon back down the embankment, unclamping the wheels of the crane vehicle, moving the train along the track for about ten yards, then starting the entire movement again. That would take fifteen to thirty minutes.

Inspector Barlowe suggested to me, 'We'll unclamp, run gently along the track for ten yards, clamp up again, then slew the jib with its wagon under the wires.'

Apart from being directly against the rules, it was absolutely sheer madness to have a wagon suspended in mid-air from the jib, then move the train with the crane along the track with the clamps disconnected. Without clamps, the lot could easily topple down the embankment. So here we go again. I spoke quietly.

'Inspector, you know as well as I do, it's irregular. Dangerous. It can't under any circumstances be done that way.'

More shouting and blustering. You would think he was about to burst a blood vessel. 'Look here, Ferney, I've done more crane jobs than you've had hot dinners. What the hell are you messing about at? How many crane jobs have you done, eh?'

I hated having to tell him. 'Only a few. And we're going to do it right!'

The chaps stood around silently, looking disgusted with the whole charade. It wasn't fair on them to be caught up in a row between their leaders, who, they would think, ought to know better. The correct and safe way took about half an hour longer.

When we came to uplift the second wagon from down the embankment, a telegraph pole was in the way of the jib by about a foot. To save time by unclamping and clamping up again, and some more shunting movements, Inspector Barlowe came up with another mad idea, even more reckless than the previous one. He said casually, as though of no consequence, 'I reckon we'll swing the jib over the down slow line. Won't take a second if we're smart.'

I reckoned that the jib, if swung round with a wagon suspended from it, would be over not only the down slow line but the up fast. And at this site we had no means of knowing whether any trains were on these lines or expected. Visibility was good for at least a mile in both directions, and certainly no train was in sight, but the inspector's suggestion was no less than criminal, and I could hardly believe it. The adrenalin was playing hell with my insides, and a big red word dripping with blood momentarily blotted out my mind – D-A-N-G-E-R!

'Inspector, that down slow line and the up fast are not protected.' I was trying hard to keep my cool, conscious that the chaps were listening and watching. 'We're certainly not going to swing that jib with a wagon on it across those lines. You know and I know, and all these men know, it would be criminal!' It was my will against his.

You'd think the fellow was about to explode. He dived his hands in his jacket pockets, produced a cigarette packet and matches and lit up a cigarette with ferocity that had to be seen to be believed. He puffed vigorously and his face went puce. I accepted that he was a man of much experience, and I half wondered whether I was just being pernickety. But all doubt quickly vanished when my imagination told me what might happen if the crane jib and its suspended wagon became stuck in mid-air above running lines and if an express came tearing along at eighty miles an hour. It was too horrific to contemplate. Sunday midday lunch would be off anyway, shattered as we would be by a crashed express.

Glowering heavily, Inspector Barlowe had to change his tactics. But the extra moves he had to make lost more time. A few minutes later an express train on the up fast line from the North came thundering into view, trailing a great plume of white steam. I stood there transfixed. It roared by, clattered past and in another minute was out of sight, the smell of steam hanging in the warm, still air. I felt cold sweat trickle down my body. My palms were clammy. The inspector avoided my gaze. I wondered what his thoughts were. His team, who had watched glassy-eyed as the express had charged by, got on with their tasks in stony silence.

Early in the afternoon our work was finished, and we climbed into the goods brake van along with the goods guard. As we chugged gently along in the reverse direction towards the Hasland signalbox, the guard, who had a twinkling face, glanced around at the glum expressions. He said, 'Let's hope we have some more wagons down the bank, then we can all come out again and get double-time on a

Sunday.' A few chuckles broke out, and they suddenly burst into helpless laughter. I couldn't avoid joining in myself, and even Inspector Barlowe's hard face cracked into smiles. As the short train shunted into the sidings at Hasland and on towards the engine sheds where the steam-crane was stationed, the mood of the men maintained a cheerful and merry note, certainly leaving us all in a state of happy relief.

During the following week, a traffic-inspector from the district office stopped me on Westhouses station where I was doing a short stint. 'I hear you had trouble with Barlowe last Sunday.'

'We had different views. But as an operating man I did my job.' I outlined the problem we had.

'That fellow must be mad. I'm amazed he's never been sacked.' We went into the empty bothy used by the shunters, and he lit his pipe. 'Let me tell you something. Last year he took the steam-crane with the breakdown train into the colliery sidings. Ten wagons of coal had run away and toppled over down the embankment. A real mess. Barlowe took his steam-crane team down there one Sunday to uplift them. D'you know, Frank, he told his steam-crane driver to lift a wagon, and the crane vehicle wasn't even clamped to the rails.'

'Oh, no, don't tell me!'

'Yes! The steam-crane with the wagon suspended from the jib tipped over. It finished up with the other wagons down there!'

'Good heavens! What about the crane-driver?'

'He jumped for his life, but he scalded his arm rather badly and had to go to hospital.'

'Thanks for telling me. I appreciate it very much. What about Barlowe? Did he get into trouble?'

'Plenty.' He paused to relight his pipe. 'A severe reprimand. By the loco superintendent at Derby HQ, no less. He was warned that the next time could be his last. But what can you do with a man like that?'

I felt the anger of last Sunday surging within. 'He should be damned-well sacked before he kills somebody!'

*

After the fracas at Hasland, I had various jobs around the
edges of my usual territory – at Burton, Birmingham,
Loughborough, Newark, Lincoln, Rotherham, Chapeltown
and a few others. While at Doe Hill, on the main line
between Nottingham and Chesterfield, I ran into a worrying
derailment.

My few staff consisted of two porters, six signalmen and a
few shunters. At two o'clock on a Saturday afternoon I
heard one ring on an electric bell on the station. That was for
me. Two short rings was the call for a porter. The bell was
operated from the signalbox a couple of hundred yards up
the line. There was no direct telephone link between station
and box. I walked carefully along the track, climbed the
steps into the signalbox and said, 'Any trouble, Bill?'

'Fraid so, sir. Six wagons off the road at Morton Sidings.
Three lines blocked. Up and down fast, and the up goods
line.' 'Up' meant towards London, the standard practice,
whether from Bradford or Brighton. I felt my heart miss a
beat and the flow of adrenalin begin. It seemed that a
shunting operation from the sidings on the down side, across
all four main lines to the sidings on the up side, had caused
the derailment. Within seconds I realized that I had a bit of a
problem on my hands. During the next few hours there
would be several express trains scheduled on both the up
and down fast lines, and a few goods trains to trundle by.

'Bill,' I said, determined to play it cool, 'that's a fine thing
to tell a fellow at two o'clock on a Saturday afternoon!'

The best way to get rid of tension in such a situation, I
have found, is to get busy. On our internal network, I
telephoned Morton Sidings signalbox for the actual time of
the derailment, how many wagons were derailed, exactly
where and what trains had been signalled to him. I also called
the control offices at Derby, Nottingham and Rotherham.
All three asked for an estimate of the length of time the lines
would be blocked. 'Difficult to say,' I told them. 'It could be
at least two or three hours.'

Profanities, quite cheerful in tone, smote my ears. One of
their problems would be to decide by which alternative
routes they would need to divert the trains. It was agreed

that a break-down train with a steam-crane would be sent
from Nottingham. The train would probably consist of flat
wagons at either side of the steam-crane to allow the jib to
swing round full circle, a wagon carrying timbers for
packing and lifting jacks, and a goods brake van with several
men aboard, including a traffic-inspector to take charge of
the re-railing operations.

Route diversions were the main problem for the control
office teams; diversions on major routes would be reflected
in some minor routes. Watching from a carriage window, the
anxious lady could be forgiven for exclaiming in a panic,
'Oh, look. The train's going the wrong way. We should have
turned left at that big junction, and we've gone to the right!'
Others would be intrigued or upset by the unaccountable
delay, finding that they had stopped in the Middle of
Nowhere.

Leaning from the window of his signalbox at a junction,
the signalman would almost certainly shout to the driver,
then the guard, 'Wagons off at Morton. We're re-routing.'
On a train, heads might peer from windows, to try to
unravel the mysteries of the railway mind. One person might
even be able to report to his fellow passengers, 'The
signalman shouted to the driver something about wagons
off to Taunton.' Another could respond, 'Taunton's in
Somerset. These railway chaps don't know what they're
doing!'

I have to confess that we on the railway were not very
good at explaining to passengers about our delays and
diversions. We were all so busy trying to get things right and
to keep the wheels turning that we forgot about the most
important person of all – the passenger.

Passengers from the North on this Saturday afternoon
would certainly be puzzled. Rotherham Control telephoned
to say that an express to London would be the first to come
our way, which meant that it would have to travel in the
wrong direction over the down goods line. 'Wrong direction'
working, as we have seen, called into play special rules, for it
was always a risky operation, requiring slow and careful
running.

The south-bound express ran steadily over the down goods line in the wrong direction to Doe Hill. At the signalbox it would have to be shunted, by running backwards over the points, onto its proper line, the up fast.

During the shunting of the train, it would need to run over points that are not interlocked with the signals because it was a goods line. On passenger lines, the regulations require that the points are interlocked with the signals. With a passenger train passing over goods points that had no interlocking, these points were required to be clipped firmly into position by a heavy iron point clip ensuring safe movement of the train.

Clipping the points was the job of the permanent-way man, but he had not yet arrived. So I was the only man available to do the job, a task I had never performed before.

Carrying the point clip from the signalbox a hundred yards or so to the points nearly killed me. It was like carrying a blacksmith's anvil. Having got the thing there, I wasn't sure how to fit it, and there was nobody to ask. Meanwhile the enormous 4-6-2 Pacific engine was blowing off steam enough to burst your ear-drums. Heads bobbed out of carriage windows of the stationary train and tried to make out what was going on. Concentration was the watchword. I put the iron point clip down on the track and knelt beside it as though in prayer. Suddenly the way it worked clicked. I placed the clip to hold the blade of the points to the main rail, then turned the small wheel as hard as I could to screw up to a firm grip. God help me if I've done it wrong.

As far as the passengers were concerned, the driver of this mighty express might have stopped to pick blackberries from the nearby hedgerow.

Meantime I gave a hand signal to the signalman at the box that the points were in order, and he turned to 'all right' the small shunting signal standing on the track side. The train began to draw slowly forward, and I climbed onto the outer steps of the engine, holding firmly to the handrails. I signalled the driver to reverse over my precious points. Curious passengers still watched. They would be able to report back to their compartments that it must be something very important, because they could see the stationmaster in his gold uniform buttons and his gold-braided cap hanging on to the side of the engine for dear life.

I gave a sigh of great relief as wheels of the train, guard's van leading, clanged over those points. I held firmly to the handrails outside the engine. Suddenly I felt a sharp pain in my right foot, as though it had been struck by something hard. At that very moment I felt myself being grabbed by strong hands, and I was literally dragged onto the footplate in the driver's cab.

'You all right, sir?'

'Yes, I think so.'

'That small shunting signal. It struck your foot. Lucky you wasn't knocked off the engine!'

By the time the train came to a stand, I was still shaking. Gingerly I climbed down the steps and onto the track, still feeling the pain in my foot. The train was shunted onto the up fast line, and curious heads receded into the comfort of the compartments. The train gathered speed as it steamed on its way to London. By that time the permanent-way man had arrived, and he took charge of the point clip and all its works, for which I was heartily glad.

In the signalbox I sat on Bill's locker, removed shoe and sock and examined the damage. Nothing much. The ankle was bleeding a little, and Bill bandaged it up, using materials from the first-aid box. I spent the next few hours there, keeping in touch with the various train movements and writing a lengthy telegram to divisional headquarters at Derby. Goods trains were held back for passenger trains.

By the early evening with the aid of the steam-crane the six derailed wagons had been lifted back onto the rails. It was with relief that I was able to write in the signalman's train register book on the next free line, 'Normal working resumed at 5.42 p.m.' and sign it. There would later be an enquiry, conducted internally, as to the exact cause of the derailment, unless the traffic-inspector in charge had been able to find the reason while on the site.

In the absence of a post office telephone at Doe Hill station, I was unable to call my wife, so I was about two hours late on arrival home in Mansfield, and I found Joan a little anxious. As I enjoyed the good meal she had prepared, I recounted the whole story. 'Let me look at that ankle,' she demanded. Yes, it's good to have a nurse in the family.

15
Chasing the Artful Fare-dodge Boys

Another promotion came my way when I was appointed to the relief stationmaster's post based at Chesterfield. Territory included lines in Derbyshire and South Yorkshire and stations on the Sheffield-Manchester route as far as Chinley, via some charming country stations on the Hope Valley line.

In my travels I came across some interesting frauds and was often astonished at public mendacity. In doing our job on the railway and checking that passengers held proper tickets, we were not really interested in the philosophy of the thing. University dons have wallowed in pages of polemics to answer the question 'Are we honest because of deep conviction or for fear of being found out?' We saw that the nicest people tried to dodge paying their railway fares, folk who would never dream of pinching a cabbage from their greengrocer or an extra pint from their milkman.

Ticket-collectors at stations and on trains came across all kinds of dodges. They became most familiar with a small segment of human psychology without really trying, and in blissful ignorance of scholars such as Freud and Jung. It's fun to listen to their stories over a convivial pint in the railway club.

A popular ploy was for the fraudulent passenger on a train to crouch behind the door in the toilet, leaving it unlocked so that the indicator on the outside shows 'vacant' instead of 'engaged'. When the ticket-man notices 'vacant', he usually goes right inside the toilet. He even looks behind the door. If it shows 'engaged', he taps politely on the door and waits. When he sees a person emerge and close the door, he thinks to himself, 'Ah, there could be another one in there, or even two.' So he enters to take a closer look.

My old friend Harold Hartly, a travelling ticket-man, described a journey from London to Manchester. When he noticed that a toilet door showed 'vacant', he pushed it

164

gently. There was obviously a foot against it. A hand came through the gap, offering a ticket. Harold inspected it, clipped it and returned it to the disembodied hand. Suspicious, he pushed hard at the door and sure enough found four more young fellows inside. In the corridor he spoke very firmly, and of course they all paid up.

'Next time,' he warned, 'I shall hand you to the police and you'll have a court case on your hands!'

We were in the club bar. Harold lifted his pint and chuckled.

'Questions, Harold, questions. How would you recognize them again? And how the devil would you get hold of the police?'

'The very mention of the police can shake 'em.'

We both knew the well-established procedure for calling the railway police when needed. Many police cases involving ticket fraud finished up in the magistrate's court.

Another common fraud was to travel without a ticket on a long journey, then tell the ticket-collector at your destination that you had joined the train at a station only a few miles back. But you have to be sure the train stopped at that nearby station. There is also the problem in the first instance of joining a train at a station where you can dodge the ticket barrier. And there is the further risk that there may be a ticket-inspector on the train itself. Such perfidy. Mother, is it worth it!

When I was acting stationmaster at Heeley, a small suburban station two miles from Sheffield main-line station, I received a call from the ticket-inspector at Sheffield.

'Did you see the 10.15 ex yours come in, Stationmaster?'

'Yes. Any problem?'

'I think so. I have a lady here in my office who says she got on the 10.15 from Heeley, but I suspect she joined the train at Derby.'

'Four people got off, and a couple of workmen got on. I'm quite sure that no lady joined the train.'

'Much obliged.'

The next time I was at Sheffield station, I saw the ticket-inspector and was told the full story.

He explained. 'The silly woman said she was visiting her sick mother in hospital and had to leave her home in Derby on short notice. Didn't have time to buy a ticket. When I said I didn't believe her, she broke down. She was so upset I couldna do owt with her.'

'Then what?'

'I took her name and address for the record from an envelope from her handbag. Then I called in the SM. Old Winfield's a good sort, you know. He said if it happened again, he would have to call the police, and no second chance. The gaffer had the authority to let her go. I didn't have. But we collected the full fare from her first.'

Passengers who travelled further than their ticket allowed were issued with an excess fare receipt when they paid up. It consisted of a small sheet of paper from the ticket-man's excess fares book, a copy of which is kept by means of carbon paper. Many people have been caught by altering the 'number of passengers' column from one to two. We had one at Codnor Park on the Erewash Valley line between Chesterfield and Nottingham. A workman gave in his excess fare ticket at the barrier for himself and a mate. But the ticket-man challenged him. 'This is for one only.'

'No, sir,' said the man. 'It's a figure two there.'

But the ticket-man knew that the carbon paper used for excess fares was double sided, and the back of the excess fare ticket clearly showed only one passenger; the figure was 1, not 2. The man had to pay up, his name and address were recorded, and he was warned it would be the police next time. It is surprising what old tricks the dodgers get up to. They forget that the ticket-man has met them all, and experience tells.

But the trick that commanded my admiration for assiduous cunning and skill was where a used but uncollected card ticket was sliced in two with a razor blade, separating the face of it from the back. The back was thrown away, and a new ticket bought for a very short journey, which had the current date stamped on the back of it. As before, the top part was sliced from the bottom part. The top part was thrown away, and the bottom part with the new date on it was stuck onto the back of the used ticket which would be for a long journey. In other words, you would glue the top of a costly ticket you had already used – say, Euston to Glasgow – to the bottom of the cheap ticket – say, Euston to Willesden – which had the new date stamped on it: a new date on an old ticket.

It was the Euston-Glasgow fraud that came to light. The cunning passenger had not been cunning enough to notice that the back of the low-priced ticket was not identical with the back of the high-priced ticket. The regulations and conditions printed in very small type were slightly different, and the grain of the cardboard of the tickets was different too. That was another case that ended with the magistrate.

When tickets on thick paper instead of cardboard began to be printed in the new glass-fronted booking-offices, it brought to an end any fancy work with razor blades.

On the LMS we were provided with a booklet about ticket irregularities and how to fox them. Included was a list of 'closed stations'. These were stations, mainly medium and large, at which ticket-collectors continuously manned the barriers. If a passenger alighted from a train without a ticket and claimed to have joined at a place listed as a 'closed station', he would certainly have some explaining to do before he could pass the ticket-collector.

While I was in the Chesterfield district, one of the most successful and regular ticket dodges I ever met was sadly perpetrated by a retired railway official. He had risen to a position that qualified him for first-class travel, and over the years he had become accustomed to its luxury and semi-privacy. Retiring at sixty, he found himself another position and journeyed about thirty miles to Sheffield daily. His free rail travel excluded residential travel, such as to and from work for another firm. This meant he needed to buy a season ticket. The silly man decided to buy a third-class season ticket but to travel first class.

But what if a travelling ticket collector was on his train? Easy! He had already bought a monthly return first-class ticket which he kept in his pocket and, if tackled, he would show his monthly return ticket instead of his third-class season. If his first-class monthly was clipped, he would buy a new one the next day.

Unfortunately for this ticket dodger, an alert booking-clerk had been watching him. He had noticed that on several occasions that although he, the booking-clerk, had issued a third-class season, the passenger entered a first-class compartment.

One morning the booking-clerk telephoned the ticket-collector at an intermediate station where the train would stop and asked him to visit the first-class compartment in mid-train. Name and address taken, the shocked fraudulent traveller was finally brought to book. I never heard the sequel, but the fellow would almost certainly have been deprived of all his free tickets and his 'privilege' travel at a quarter fare for the rest of his days – and, if he were married, those for his wife as well.

In my temporary lodgings in Chesterfield, at home with a friendly middle-aged couple, the husband was a commercial traveller. For his samples he used a hamper which he would send in advance to, say, Bradford or York, where it would remain in the railway station left-luggage office. For a week this would be his base, collecting specific samples and taking them to prospective customers around the city. He enjoyed the facilities of specially reduced fares and left-luggage charges available to commercial travellers on showing their membership cards of the commercial travellers' association.

Sitting in their tidy front room one evening, I heard a smattering of conversation and quiet chuckles between man and wife coming from the kitchen. We all know that, if you listen in to other folks' private chatter, you rarely hear anything good about yourself. A hoarse male whisper reached my keen ears. 'Don't let that railway blighter know!' I gathered he was explaining with some glee a railway ticket fiddle with a colleague in a system he seemed to claim was foolproof. On other evenings I caught the drift of similar talk but could never fathom the details. Sometimes he would ask me for a good train on a particular route, but he never enquired about the fares.

At times I felt like tackling him about the supposed

fiddling, but I had no hard evidence. Even if I had, would I have sounded him? I could have done, on the premise that he would be caught sooner or later, possibly with serious results. Rationalizing, I could thus be helping him! Had we have clashed on the issue, it would have ended our friendly association and deprived me of very pleasant lodgings. What frail creatures we are, to be sure!

Peter Collat, a travelling ticket-man based at Chesterfield, told me how he himself was caught out on a train to London. Entering the compartment from the corridor, his keen eye spotted furtive glances, but on inspection he found the tickets of the few passengers in order. Then, about to return to the corridor, he thought he heard a voice call, 'Lemme out, lemme out!' Immediately he was suspicious of a large trunk occupying much of the floor. Something ridiculous here, he thought. So he politely requested the owner, 'Please open the trunk, sir.'

'It's not what you …'

'Please, sir, open it.'

He did. It was empty. The laugh was on Peter when the bulky package held on the lap of an old lady seated in the corner proved to be housing an indignant talking parrot.

On a stopping train to Leeds, Peter entered a compartment and a lady showed her ticket, then that of her terrier dog at her feet. On the opposite seat, with her mother, sat a little girl, who now began to cry. Gently, Peter asked her, 'Why are you crying, missie?'

The little lass opened a carrier-bag and showed him a furry kitten. 'Pussie hasn't got a ticket.'

'Well, we'll soon put that right for you, missie.' In his excess fares book, he wrote out a paper ticket and handed it to the mother.

'That'll be a shilling, please.'

She looked surprised but paid it up without a query.

'My own ticket only cost 10d,' she told him.

He assured her it was correct and explained, 'Animals are charged on a zoning basis and one shilling is the minimum, I'm afraid, madam.'

Problems for ticket-collectors often arise with schoolchildren. They are positively gifted at losing their season tickets, and this gives enormous scope to their youthful imagination. 'I left it in my other jacket, sir,' or, 'I must have dropped it somewhere.'

Peter Collat tells how one afternoon he found a boy who had mislaid his ticket trying the artful dodge of using his friend's. Even that let him down, for it was a week out of date. One day Peter came across a boy in the train who had mislaid his ticket in a most novel way. He had dropped it in the gap into which the window of the door was raised or lowered.

'I haven't really lost it,' the boy protested. 'I can still see it.'

'So can I,' said Peter. 'But the point is that I can't inspect it!'

And yet another tale. On a non-stop train between Chesterfield and Sheffield, he found a girl and a fellow in a compartment by themselves.

'Tickets, please,' he called.

The girl handed him hers, from Chesterfield to Sheffield. Looking very uncomfortable, the fellow handed him a penny platform ticket. He explained that he had sat for a moment in the train with his girl at Chesterfield, intending to get off before it started.

'I'll want the fare to Sheffield, sir,' Peter told him. 'Why didn't you hop off before it started?'

'I tried to. But look what happened.'

Unbelievably, his trouser leg had been trapped in the door. Poor lad! At Sheffield he would need to buy another ticket back to Chesterfield.

Another couple who caused a stir were a stage further along love's dream. They were off on their honeymoon. The compartment was pretty full, and the shy groom handed a note to Peter asking if there were an empty compartment further along the train. Peter went along the corridor to see and, returning, beckoned the young couple to follow.

In the corridor the groom, somewhat self-conscious, dropped a case on a lady's toe. Turning red, he apologized. Part way along the corridor, even more embarrassed, he realized that he had left his hat behind on the rack. Finally the procession of three began to move along again. Now, suddenly, there was a long, continuous ringing from a hold-all, and people in each compartment stared as the three moved unsteadily by. Some joker of a wedding guest must have planted an alarm-clock in the hapless groom's luggage.

On that same train Peter entered a full compartment in which a young woman loaded with parcels was holding a baby on her lap. She hunted and fumbled, went through purse and pocket but still couldn't find her ticket. Distracted, she handed the baby to Peter to hold.

He recalls, 'I was a bit clumsy holding that baby but, bless her, she gave me a lovely smile and said, "Da-da". You can imagine the chuckles from the passengers.' Chuckles turned to loud laughter when the baby handed him the lost ticket, wet and well chewed, much to the young mother's embarrassment.

Finally, back to fare-dodgers. Why do so many come unstuck? I believe they have no deep perception of the reality that a ticket-inspector dealing with people and tickets day in and day out must get to know all the possible variations on any dodging theme. Yet still they keep on trying.

16

Putting the Bottoms on the Seats

Soon after the war I was promoted to sales representative for passenger train business – people and parcels – and was based at Sheffield. Our office, called 'The Farm', was an ancient dark stone edifice, once a country mansion, several minutes' walk from the station.

Mr Heath, the chief clerk, was a charming man, fiftyish, with ears that stuck out like open taxi doors. 'Your job, my dear chap,' said Mr Heath, 'is to get bottoms on seats.' My territory was half the city and the Hope Valley line that burrowed beneath the Pennines through an extremely long tunnel towards Manchester.

One of my functions was to seek out group travel. To this end I visited clubs and societies of all kinds, to put on film shows of railway travel. Audiences included scout groups, Sunday schools and churches, Band of Hope temperance groups, trade and business associations, schools, women's organizations and professional societies in and around the city.

An evening's programme would usually include my introductory talk, screening two or three travel films, then questions. Youngsters were most interested in steam-locomotives and fast expresses, especially trains with their own names. To add to the entertainment, we had scrounged a few old silent films: Charlie Chaplin and Buster Keaton, Laurel and Hardy, Harold Lloyd, and Douglas Fairbanks and Mary Pickford.

During the many trips I initiated in my six months in the Sheffield job, some piquant situations arose. A big steelworks in the city, Firthly Brown, asked me to call on their social secretary, as we were planning evening trips to Blackpool at ten shillings a time to see the incredible array of coloured lights along miles of the sea front.

Mr Jones invited me to take a seat. A clerk, I thought.

Medium build and rather meek in style. He couldn't have been much older than me. He began, 'Our people would like to go on one of your Blackpool evening trips, to see the lights. We'd like to take our own cases of beer.'

'That's fine, Mr Jones. How many want to go?'

'Difficult to say, really. Could be two hundred.'

'Right.'

My salesmanship antennae began to vibrate. 'The sooner you book, Mr Jones, the better choice you'll have of the train times. Going there and coming back.'

'I'll enquire. I'll put a notice on the staff board. Can I let you know next week?'

'Why not a firm booking today? Now?'

That seemed to shock the fellow. He hesitated. 'Oh, I don't really know about that.'

'Look, our trains can take over four hundred. That would be an exclusive to Firthly Brown. Let's take a chance and book a train for you.'

'Oh, golly gosh. I don't know really.'

'Could you guarantee, say, a hundred?'

'Oh, easily.'

'Right. Let me book a complete train for your firm, and if you can't fill it, I can easily, with other parties. So you take absolutely no risk.'

'Well, OK then.'

'Good man. Can I use your phone? Oh, thanks.'

I called my office. 'Will you book a train, exclusive for Mr Jones of Firthly Brown, Bill? Good. 15 September. Yes, for the lights. Suggested timings to follow. OK? Thanks, Bill.' I turned to my client. 'Mr Jones, sir, you now have your own train.'

'Good heavens!'

'I'll come and see you next Monday. And if all your people say "no", I can easily sell the whole train to some other firm. So you've nothing to worry about, Mr Jones.'

He took out his handkerchief and wiped his brow, and I left him. Next Monday I called on the gentleman as promised. Surprise, surprise, he was bright and perky. 'We've got over five hundred. I'm staggered!'

'May I use your phone?'

'Gosh, yes.'

'Hallo, Bill? That you, Bill? Frank here. Will you book another train for Mr Jones? Thanks. I'll leave you to fix the name boards. What? Yes, for the front of the engines. Call them "Firthly Brown's Blackpool Special". OK? 'Bye.'

You should have seen Mr Jones' face. 'Who's paying for the name boards?'

'On the house, Mr Jones. On the house!'

Nearly nine hundred people went to Blackpool on Mr Jones' two trains, together with many cases of beer. And a good time was had by all.

Meanwhile I went canvassing other firms prodigiously for trips to Blackpool to see the lights, while it was still topical. So during that autumn a lot of fellers like me, within shouting distance of the Lancashire resort, were responsible for cluttering up the streets of Blackpool, vastly increasing the consumption of fish and chips and beer and filling a few more police cells with inhabitants for a one-night stand. Analysing the philosophy of the thing, I cogitated on how I could remain in the railway service, with its marvellous steam trains, and serve the community in general to a more socially desirable advantage.

One of my trips was for a Sheffield school. The schoolmaster and two assistants took thirty-six boys to London for a day out.

To make their journey more interesting, I provided the schoolmaster in advance with a list, which he had had duplicated, of things to see from the carriage windows. Among them were towns and villages, landmarks, unusual churches and, of course, the famous crooked spire at Chesterfield. My notes said that warped timbers had gradually put the steeple in a twist. Items to look out for on the track side included stations, signalboxes, telegraph poles carrying wires for telegraph and telephone messages; small boards which showed the gradients of the line; and the mileposts, on the left side of the line going south, showing the distance from London at every quarter of a mile, Sheffield being 164. Another note explained how any schoolboy could estimate the speed of the train by counting

the number of rail joints they passed in forty-one seconds.
The answer gave the miles per hour.

I was on the platform as the reserved carriage filled up
with laughing, chattering lads. Among the many parents
who saw their offspring to the station, one mother asked the
schoolmaster, 'How many in the party?'

'Thirty-six, Mrs Birch, exactly.'

She grinned sheepishly. 'You won't lose any, will you?'

'I don't expect so. There are three of us in charge, and
we've done lots of outings over the years. Don't worry, my
dear. We count them off the train, on or off tube trains and
buses, in and out of cafés and museums. Rest assured, we
have a good system.' But there was something he hadn't
counted on.

Steam billowing, the train drew away from the platform to
a forest of waving hands, and calls of, 'Goodbye, and keep
out of trouble!'

In the Sheffield office, some days later, I had a phone call
from the schoolmaster. 'I doubt if you'll believe this.'

'Try me, sir.'

I could hear him chortling. 'We checked the number of
boys at every stage. You know, the usual pattern. At every
place we visited. And thirty-six boys got off the train at
Sheffield. But two mums were crazy with worry because
their boys weren't there. One was the lad named Birch.'

'Yet thirty-six boys had returned?'

'That's right. But we found we had mislaid two of ours
and had acquired two cockney lads, brothers, instead.'

'The plot thickens!'

He enjoyed that. 'The cockney boys learned at St Pancras
that we were a Sheffield party, so the cheeky blighters tacked
on to visit an aunt in Sheffield.'

You couldn't help smiling.

'So,' the schoolmaster added, 'we had to send a telegram to
their mother in London. And our two missing lads arrived in
Sheffield on the next train.'

'What kept them?'

'Gambling on the pin-tables in Soho. In an amusement
arcade!'

Such debauchery for innocent boys from Sheffield in the

wicked metropolis was better withheld from their adoring mothers.

As a job, creating and arranging group travel was always rewarding. It was always different, always changing. You were supplying people of all ages and types with something pleasurable. But occasionally things went wrong, and a few people naturally complained.

Depending on the number travelling in a party, we allowed a proportion of free tickets for those who supervised the actual journey or visited in advance the venue to plan the day, weekend or longer period. Sometimes an outing to London included visits to museums, a coach run, a river trip, a restaurant meal, a theatre. Then there were visits to places such as Madame Tussaud's or the Tower of London, where you paid to go in and estimated your time of arrival. A couple of party leaders would be able to travel without charge days or weeks in advance to 'case the joint' and to tie up the details.

Much of my contribution consisted of advice: how to get there and what there is to do on arrival. We took into account the weather and the seasons. Occasionally I would go on one of the outings to see at first hand what went on, especially if there were complications. Outings in which I was involved included Edinburgh, Glasgow and other Scottish centres, the Yorkshire and the Derbyshire dales and the Lake District. Popular trips included Liverpool, to see famous ocean-going liners and to ride on the ferry across the Mersey to New Brighton, and Grimsby and Hull, busy with the shipping lines to Europe.

Enginemen and guards, most of them dads themselves, were always ready to chat with the children. Occasionally a brave boy would be allowed to climb onto the footplate alongside the driver, where he would feel the heat of the furnace and smell the steam and oil. At that peak of excited emotion, the defenceless boy might be captivated by the mysterious magic of steam trains, never able to escape from its enchantment.

A guard sometimes allowed children to join him for a few minutes in his van. He would show them the switches for the

Frank Ferneyhough and a friend about to embark on a footplate
ride on the *Atlantic Coast Express*.

For years bright scarlet chocolate machines were popular on stations. A station employee stocked the machines and earned twopence in the shilling commission for his trouble.

Coffee blending in the cellars beneath St Pancras station – a longstanding daily ritual.

This highly-decorated railway policeman's truncheon bears the name Birmingham and the figures 89 – presumably part of 1889. It came to light at Cheddington, Bucks, in the early 1960s.

CHESHIRE LINES
NOTICE
THESE CLOSETS ARE INTENDED FOR THE CONVENIENCE OF PASSENGERS ONLY, WORKMEN, CABMEN, FISHPORTERS AND PEDLERS ARE NOT PERMITTED TO USE THEM. BY ORDER

Various public notices have appeared on railway premises over the years. Here's one that really puts the idlers in their place!

This unique memorial at Bromsgrove near Worcester honours
two distinguished railway officers. Thomas Scaife was killed at
the station by an engine boiler exploding, a common event in
pioneering days.

Every now and again a train
does run a little late . . .!

One of O.V. Bulleid's fancy locomotives in the Leader class. A tank engine built in 1949 at Brighton Works, Southern Region, it was an 0-6-6-0 with two bogies, each with six coupled wheels and three cylinders. Found to be unsuitable after trial running, it was soon withdrawn.

The body of Sir Winston Churchill was conveyed on this train from London to Handborough in 1965, for the burial at Bladon Church within sight of Blenheim Palace, Churchill's birthplace.

Never get a billy-goat's goat unless you're well padded! (*see Chapter 2*).

'It's no good crying over spilt milk, my kitties – just get started!' (*see Chapter 8*).

WANTED
EMPTY WAGONS!

REWARD
A PAYLOAD FOR EVERY ONE REPORTED!

THERE'S A JOB—AND EARNING POWER—WAITING FOR EVERY EMPTY WAGON.
BUT YOU DON'T KNOW WHERE THE JOB IS—AND UNLESS YOU REPORT THEM
CONTROL DOESN'T KNOW WHERE THE EMPTIES ARE!

KEEP THOSE WAGONS WORKING!

ISSUED BY BRITISH RAILWAYS CENTRAL WAGON AUTHORITY

2B

'Eh, you – get those wagons working!' This eye-catching poster
of the 1930s was part of a national campaign to cut the waste of
wagons.

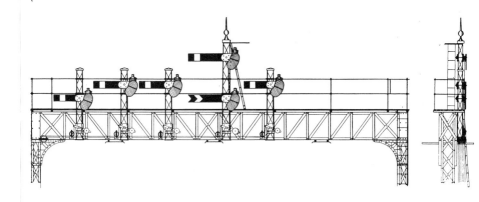

A typical signal gantry between the wars. All were lit by oil-lamps, the oil being replenished weekly by a signal lampman.

Swindon-built in 1960, *Evening Star* was the very last steam locomotive to be built by British Railways. It is now preserved in the National Railway Museum at York.

electric lights throughout the train. He would explain the big wheel that worked a handbrake on his van. He would point out the handle that works the vacuum brake throughout the entire train. He would show them the tools he keeps for emergency, his first-aid box and other equipment which, for such young minds, he would prefer not to dwell upon. The children would be able to look through the rear window to see the track whizzing away from them at a dizzy pace.

Guard Henry Jackson was a good friend of mine. He wore a mischievous face and was Dad to five mischievous children. We were chatting in his van in a train that was on a school trip to Manchester. We had left Sheffield about three minutes when he said, 'Would you like a bit of fun?'

'Sure, Henry. I *always* like a bit of fun.'

'Stand by the corridor there. In a few minutes, you'll hear the most almighty scream what ever struck your ears!'

'I can't believe it. Who will scream?'

'Why, the kids o' course.'

'But why will they scream?'

'Shock. That's why. And a touch of fear.' He was grinning at me now.

'Come on, Henry. Is this some joke or something? And you a family man. Gosh, you can see the headlines in the *Sheffield Telegraph*: "Railway Guard Terrifies Children on Manchester Express".'

Just for a moment he looked serious. Then his cheery grin appeared again. 'It' don't do no harm. I done it on me own kids.'

Then, suddenly, there was the most almighty scream. I realized that we had just plunged with a deafening roar into Dore Tunnel. The lights in the guard's van were still on. I noticed he had his hand on a switch, and I realized he had allowed his train to roar into the darkened tunnel for some seconds before switching on all the train lights. We both had a good laugh.

One of the joys of children's outings was to see their innocent faces and hear their uninhibited merriment. In their eyes was a real sense of wonder and excitement and adventure. I still have sharp memories of short trips on steam trains along our local branch line in north Staffordshire to some favourite beauty spot. Ah, me! Wonderful times.

In my early twenties I had given the occasional talk and, when attending public meetings, forced myself, despite distracting fluttering butterflies, to ask a question. At first the idea frightened me to death. In anticipation I could feel my tummy rolling round, was aware of my face flushing bright red and found I was breathing as though I had just run up a steep hill. While at Sheffield I discovered that I had a natural propensity for public performances, an ability to make an audience laugh and to provoke plenty of discussion. It brought much fun and pleasure for me, modest new business to the LMS Railway, and added to my fund of amusing vignettes which, from time to time, amused others as well.

While working in Sheffield I was still living in Mansfield. Bus and train, plus some walking, took an hour and a half each way. On those evenings when I gave a film show or a public talk, I often reached home as late as nine or even ten at night. Then up at six the next morning for another daily round. Fees from the film shows and talks compensated a little, but on such jaunts I missed those family romps with my kids.

One pleasant side of my job at Sheffield was that, in organizing village groups on outings, I was able to visit some of the country stations on the Hope Valley line. When I was earmarked for a writing post on the LMS in London, I reflected on the years I had spent at small stations on branch lines: Staffordshire, Cheshire, Derbyshire, Nottinghamshire, Lincolnshire, Cambridgeshire, Yorkshire, Leicestershire, Bedfordshire, Northamptonshire, Buckinghamshire, Oxfordshire, Hertfordshire, Middlesex – I had worked in all these counties.

My stays were mainly short but often repeated. I found that stations at villages and small towns, with their local steam trains, did more than provide services for passengers and goods. Most were an intrinsic part and a focal point for the community. Each area had its own topography and natural history, its own legends and folklore, and often its own special attractions for public visitors.

Station staff, in or out of uniform, were familiar and respected figures and were oft-times at the heart of local life and activities. They served on local councils, parent-teacher associations and church councils, took part in music and drama, helped with the local fêtes, horticultural shows and gymkhanas, and joined the locals on outings to places of interest.

The stationmaster ranked as a citizen of repute, along with the school headmaster, vicar, family doctor and other professionals and businessmen. He belonged to the Rotarians or to the local Chamber of Commerce or served on the local sports committees for cricket or football, bowls or tennis. Sometimes he became mayor of the town and would join other railwaymen mayors at a reception by the directors at LMS Railway headquarters in London.

No invitation list for local functions would be complete without the stationmaster's name, and if his station served a local 'big house', the squire would send him a brace of pheasants at Christmas, and his bailiff might deliver a couple of rabbits for the pot now and again. On his station platforms he would touch his peaked cap and greet regular passengers by name. He was proud of his calling and carried a loyalty to the railway that he would hold for life. Always he was keen to maintain punctual running of the trains and to supervise the prompt and careful loading and unloading of merchandise of all kinds.

Frequently the stationmaster and his staff would make delightful station gardens perfumed by roses and wallflowers, and join with other stations in an annual station garden competition. Prizes would include the means of purchasing more seeds, plants and shrubs, and reports would appear in the local newspaper and in the LMS Railway staff magazine.

Local places of call such as the village post office, the Horse and Hound pub and the village stores were centres of friendly gossip and chat about personal and family affairs. Yes, I knew I was going to miss the warmth of country railway folks. I would miss the local postmen as they came to the station in their red vans to load and unload their bags of mail, the cheep-cheep of day-old chicks in their specially ventilated cartons, the loading of racehorses and cattle, despatching fruit and vegetables to the markets by train, the clang-clang of milk churns being loaded up by the farmer for despatch to the large dairy companies, the smell of new-mown hay in the nearby meadows, and parties of country children going on a trip by train for a day's romp. And with it all, nature's constant changes throughout the four seasons. Country people always seemed to be very much at home, rooted near their relations and wrapping their village or market town around themselves like an old, patched-up coat.

But, inevitably for me, the Great Metropolis called. Perhaps I would be able to make a family home in a country village or a small town, one with its own railway station and a reliable steam-train service to take me to and from my work.

17
Steam to Stay on Britain's Railways!

Those six months spent, as a stranger, in the Sheffield district among such friendly and helpful folks were memorable, and still in the heyday of steam trains. After that, I was promoted temporarily to the London headquarters of the LMS Railway. My new task was to write a standard textbook entitled *Booking and Parcels Office Clerical Work*, which also included the accounting systems.

Though the textbook job was only a 'one-off', I began to feel that I would find the best scope for my very modest skills in the Great Metropolis. The textbook was, in fact, later adopted by British Railways after nationalization in 1948 and was in use until 1970, when station accountancy was radically changed.

State ownership created the British Transport Commission, the policy-making body for all the transport services – railways, ships, British road services, London Transport, provincial and Scottish buses, hotels, catering, docks and inland waterways. Against much competition, I secured the post of writer for staff publications. I had two books behind me, and numerous articles published in magazines and newspapers. This, plus an intimate knowledge of the railways, apparently gave me the edge.

Though I was called upon to write about all the services, much of my output was about the railways. I thus combined two superb hobbies – railways and writing. Plus a private office, plus first-class travel, plus the chance to choose St Albans for our new home. Twenty miles from St Pancras on the Midland main line and served by an excellent system of steam trains, it was a civilized place to live in, to put down roots and to bring up the children. We became so involved in the life of the town that to leave it was unthinkable, promotion or not. And by a fluke in 1951 my wife and I were to start a retail office-equipment business, employing four or five people and selling out after twenty years.

My job as a staff writer brought a fair amount of travel. This, in turn, led to many amusing experiences of the oddities in railway travel.

Among the staff I got to know was Eddie Bonnett. In some ways a quixotic character, he shared my love of the great steam-locomotives such as the *Royal Scots* and the *Gresley Pacifics*. Always smart and tidy, Eddie was the chief steward on dining-cars on the King's Cross-Newcastle-Edinburgh route. Tall and slim, he parted his hair in the centre and sported a brindled moustache which he waxed at the ends, sergeant-major fashion.

Often on my travels north in the early 1950s I found myself on his train and enjoyed his peculiar sense of fun. One of the continuous problems for Eddie, or indeed anyone in the fickle train catering business, is – how many ravenous humans will want lunch or dinner, breakfast or afternoon tea? Train caterers worked closely with their section managers located at main stations. There, food and drink were taken aboard, often from huge hampers, their tiny wheels squealing as they were hauled along the platforms from the catering stores by the dining-car steward.

Eddie had a good reputation in the department for estimating closely to passengers' needs, thus reducing waste. Some said he had a secret, an authentic and infallible system, a formula he would keep to himself.

Finishing my lunch on the Edinburgh express one day, I tried to persuade him yet again. 'Come on, Eddie. Be a pal. What's your secret?'

He hesitated. 'Tell you what. When we've cleared the tables, I'll show you in my private compartment. Confidential, mind you!'

Half an hour later I joined him. He bolted his door. From the pocket of his mufti jacket hanging on a coat hanger, he produced with a flourish in the style of a conjuror a small glass orb as big as a tennis ball. Its gaudy streaks of colour in the gamut of the spectrum caught the light most arrestingly.

'That's it, Mr Ferney,' he grinned, speaking quietly. 'My crystal ball.'

This, I thought, was far beyond the bounds of plausibility. 'Eddie, don't be ridiculous. You can't be serious, man!'

'Never more serious in my life.'

Through the window, I gazed at the passing meadows speeding by. I wanted to reassure myself that there was a real world out there. 'Tell me about it.'

Suddenly quiet, he sat at his tiny table, placed the sphere of glass on an empty brass ashtray, put his hands to his forehead like some eastern prophet, then concentrated. Changing scenery still flashed by the window, and the ordinary noises of the steam train could still be heard. With a piercing scream of the engine whistle, the train roared into a short tunnel. It made me jump, but Eddie remained frozen in concentration as if in a trance. In daylight once more, he began to mumble.

'Eh, come on, Eddie. Cut out the comic stuff and let's get down to brass tacks!'

He looked up at me, glared, then resumed his concentration.

After a few minutes, he muttered, 'Two families joining at Newcastle, and a little old lady with an umbrella ... several businessmen ... and a middle-aged American with a large hat. Then those on the train going all the way to Edinburgh. That'll be ... first class ... third class ... Thirty-nine for dinner.' He picked up the sphere, polished it lovingly with a yellow duster, returned it to his pocket, gave me a sly wink, then reminded me, 'Confidential, mind you!'

He unbolted the door and made off towards the kitchen car. By his small table on the floor, I spotted a scrap of paper. I picked it up. Scribbled in pencil were notes of numbers of passengers at start of journey assessed by the King's Cross catering head office, plus a few regulars joining at Newcastle, plus random diners – estimated total, thirty-nine. It all confirmed what a load of old rubbish that crystal ball was.

In the dining-car, when dinner was over, somewhere north of the Scottish border, Eddie gave me my bill. I asked him, 'How many for dinner?'

He grinned smugly. 'Thirty-seven.'

'Brilliant! You'd estimated thirty-nine. You deserve top marks.'

'Thanks, Mr Ferney. My crystal ball's absolutely marvellous. Never lets me down.'

Then he went about his business.

As I was leaving the train at Edinburgh Waverley station, I spotted Eddie at the door of the kitchen car. I handed him that scrap of paper. 'I found it on the floor,' I explained. 'It must have dropped out of your crystal ball.'

On another occasion I was travelling back from Manchester on a mid-morning express for Euston. Passing into Hertfordshire, I walked along the corridor to the toilet compartment. The indicator on the door showed 'engaged'. I waited awhile, then heard knocking as though from the inside. I tapped in response, like a spy in a mystery story. The knocking became louder, more persistent. I tapped again. Faintly, I heard a lady's voice. 'I'm locked in. Can't get out.' A pause, then, 'I've been here ages. And I've just pulled the communication cord.' The panicky voice sounded elderly.

I heard our express locomotive ease off her power. The train began to reduce speed, accompanied by a squeal of brake blocks on carriage wheels.

Meantime I hurried along to the guard's van, which happened to be the next vehicle. It was strewn with parcels and mailbags. The guard had realized the communication cord must have been pulled, and I was able to fill in the details. At that moment we plunged with a whoosh into Watford tunnel, which I knew was a little north of Watford station. As the communication cord gives only a partial braking, the driver would aim to run his train into a platform at Watford. With a small lever the guard tried to prise open the door of the toilet. By now the train had stopped, and the stationmaster arrived to say that other trains following behind were being held up. The guard nipped smartly out onto the platform and turned the tell-tale disc indicator which was fixed at roof level. His action released the vacuum brake and he signalled the driver to start. Back on the train, he called to the marooned passenger and explained what was happening.

I didn't see how he finally loosened the door, but he managed to squeeze his hand through the narrow gap to release the lock on the inside of the door. The embarrassed lady stepped into the corridor, profoundly relieved and profusely apologetic. Neatly dressed, she couldn't have been a fraction over five feet tall. 'I don't mind paying a fine. It was my silly fault entirely,' she offered.

Our guard examined the door lock and found it was working but was very stiff.

'No need for that, madam,' he assured her, smiling. 'It were our fault. That door bolt were real hard. But,' he added kindly, 'I'll want your name and address for my report.'

We ran the final $17\frac{1}{2}$ miles from Watford at a hell of a lick and reached Euston only fourteen minutes late.

Living in St Albans and working in London converted me into a commuter, a word which we seemed recently to have imported from America. Six of us customarily sat in a compartment together. Monty Fitzroy-Smith was one. You looked at him and said to yourself: though as yet only an insignificant clerk with big ideas, he is 'something in the city' personified. Large, expensive briefcase, pink *Financial Times*, black jacket and striped trousers, navy-blue Cromby overcoat, Homburg hat, pale face and a thin moustache, William Powell style.

It was a hard winter. Snow lay thick upon the ground. In such weather Monty would walk to the station in his wellingtons. He would jump into the train, whip off the wellingtons smartly, then hand them through the open carriage door to the obliging, waiting porter, to whom he would give a handsome tip. (On his return in the evening, a porter would have the wellingtons ready for him.) As the morning train steamed off, he would produce from his briefcase a pair of city shoes and place them on his feet. Now he would exchange commuter smalltalk with us for a few social minutes and finally bury himself deeply and anxiously in the *Financial Times*.

This particular morning Monty had cut it fine. He only

just managed to scramble into the train. It was due to leave at 8.20 a.m. to cover the twenty-mile journey in twenty-five minutes. We all knew that he had taken his wife to a late dance the night before. As usual he carried out his wellingtons routine, handing them out to the waiting porter and not forgetting to tip him.

Our usual party settled into our usual daily places. The guard blew his whistle, and the train was away. We exchanged our customary greetings and pleasantries of the kind you could have heard in commuter trains anywhere on the railway network, before settling to our daily newspapers.

Monty opened his expensive briefcase. Suddenly he exploded, 'Oh, hell!' and continued with a flow of expletives not heard in polite society, though possibly quite acceptable in the Billingsgate and Smithfield markets. He produced from his briefcase, for all of us to see – a pair of pink satin, high-heeled dancing shoes. He thrust them back angrily.

We tried to concentrate on the bad news of the day, but visions of Monty walking into his City office without any shoes on made some of us titter. Then Freddie Bowles broke the spell of silence and dropped his *Daily Telegraph* on the floor, threw back his head and laughed loud and long. We others had no choice but to join him. Monty glared and growled. Inevitably, he also saw the funny side and soon was howling with laughter louder than any of us.

When the train reached the terminus, Monty sat forlornly in his dark grey socks as the rest of us began to leave the train. Plaintively he said to me, 'You're not going to leave me stranded in my desperate hour of need, surely?'

You could have been forgiven for thinking that his ship was going down.

'Of course not, old chap. I'll call a porter,' and I hailed one with a pair of good shoulders.

Passengers in a hurry to get to work were surging by. A few eyebrows were raised and people smiled at the sight that met their eyes. Even Monty grinned laconically as he was carried, shoeless, on the broad back of the hefty porter along the shiny wet platform towards the St Pancras station taxi-rank.

Among our commuter friends, we all had many laughs as

we told and retold the details of this comic incident. And in the telling, it graduated rapidly from the whimsical to the purely chimerical.

In our department at headquarters, we were concerned with publications, publicity and the Press; we were always conscious of the need for sound English, accuracy, lucidity and a sensible word-economy. Ordinary railway departmental circular letters were often loquacious and imprecise. After Sir Ernest Gowers had published his book *Plain Words*, somebody at HQ sent a circular encouraging the writers of them to study that author. Clear instructions, it emphasized, especially those about carriage and locomotive workings, goods train and marshalling yard schedules and other detailed operations, were most essential.

One morning a circular letter landed on my desk. It was addressed to 'All Heads of Sections'. It showed the sender as the Chief Business Operations – Policy Officer, British Railways Headquarters, complete with date, reference number and the internal telephone extension. Here is the letter:

OUTGOING CORRESPONDENCE

From a check of carbon copies of outgoing correspondence, it is clear that there are many members of staff who are finding it difficult to manipulate their jargon in such a way as to maintain the illusion that they have something important or meaningful to say. With this in mind, the following tables have been produced.

When one is stuck for an effectively contemporary phrase [*sic*], one simply chooses a three digit number and then looks up the corresponding words in the table. Table A is to be used for internal correspondence, Table B for external. Nine times out of ten, the resultant phrase will be suitable; for example, A 610, 467, and B 011, 604. These tables should be used only as and when necessary, otherwise you may end up kidding yourself.

for T.W. ROYLE
   [initialled]

(T.W. Royle was a former chief operating manager of the LMS.)

TABLE A

1. total	1. duo-rail	1. analog
2. non linear	2. third generation	2. spinoffs
3. multidisciplinary	3. on line	3. parameters
4. in depth	4. corporate	4. software
5. intra urban	5. multilinear	5. program(me)
6. perceived	6. environmental	6. methodology
7. pragmatic	7. nodal	7. feedback
8. outmoded	8. organisational	8. threshold
9. responsible	9. digital	9. imponderables
0. surplus	0. ancillary	0. options

TABLE B

1. dynamic	1. lateral	1. thinking
2. significant	2. academic	2. awareness
3. creative	3. notional	3. commitment
4. open ended	4. socio-political	4. response
5. meaningful	5. structural	5. perspective
6. relevant	6. Euro-	6. community
7. collective	7. cultural	7. reference
8. contemporary	8. ambivalent	8. participation
9. integrated	9. evolutionary	9. continuum
0. systematised	0. consumer	0. freedom

The circular ended: 'Please ensure that all staff in your department see this.'

I must be a bit thick, because it wasn't until the second reading that I noticed the reference UR/A/1-2 and the date – 1 April.

In our department, which was concerned mainly with the image of the railways, we were expected to play down steam when the new diesels and electrics took over. But gradually our top people began to see the commercial value of steam trains and allowed the railway societies to run a limited number of private steam specials. Later they sponsored some of their own steam-hauled excursions.

As a steam enthusiast, I often came in for some legpull by colleagues, and I quote an example.

Let's call him Guy Parkes, to preserve our friendship. He

was one of the bright young executives snapped up during the Beeching regime. A sparkling clean face exuding an aromatic drift of a strong after-shave lotion. Sleek black hair and well-pressed city clothes. Though originally trained as a diesel engineer, at British Rail he now worked on something deeply mysterious and highly suspect called 'cybernetics'. I couldn't help wondering what cybernetics was doing to our fare-paying passengers and whether it was catching.

At headquarters in the management restaurant, waitress-served and alive with about eighty at lunch, Guy regularly joined our table for six, because, he said, he was 'intrigued by the charming and frivolous loquacity of public relations department wordmongers'. We have been called worse.

As a non-railwayman, he was sure that many railway notions were screamingly out of date. Over a meal he would exclaim, 'Every time I look at you, Frank, I hear firebox doors clang open and feel the heat of the engine furnace scorching my face.'

Colleague Charles chipped in, 'Didn't think you felt *anything*, Guy. I'd say there's a diesel engine where your heart ought to be!'

'Compliments I ignore, old boy. Look, why be steambound? Steam, like the Dodo, is dead.' He poked at his pork chop. 'Diesels and electrics are quick and clean. Steam blacks up the stations and the carriage door-handles. And the chimney chucks dirty great smuts in your eye if you dare to have the window open.'

Charles laughed. 'Eh, Guy, sure you want to work for the railways?'

'Sure, to modernize you lot. Look, it's 1964 now. I'll bet British Railways won't be running any more regular steam trains within, say, five years.'

'Right,' I said, 'make it a fiver. And I'll see you in 1969!'

'Done,' said Guy, and we shook hands on it. 'By the way, I passed your ancient monument of a station at St Albans yesterday. Smelly, puttering gas lighting. I couldn't believe it.'

'We're having a new station sometime.'

'I could believe that.'

I told him, 'Gas-lit carriages ran until the 1950s. And we've at least sixteen carriages running on BR with no artificial lighting at all.'

'Not even oil?'

'No. But it's the best system of lighting that's been discovered so far.'

'Tell me.'

'Daylight.' Our chaps at the lunch table enjoyed that. 'They're on the Rheidol Valley line from Aberystwyth. Marvellous little railway.'

Guy tried the needle again. 'Horsedrawn?'

'No. Steam!'

Time to change tack. He talked about his career. Liverpool University, then training at Newton in Lancashire. I reminded him that he owed his training to the steam-engine and Robert Stephenson, son of the famous George who was known as 'the father of railways'.

'How come? We made diesels and electrics at Vulcan.'

'But it used to be steam-engines. That works was founded as a joint venture by Charles Tayleur and Robert Stephenson in 1832.'

'They never told *me*!'

He enjoyed his little quip, then invited me for a quick pint at a pub he knew. I might have known. It was the Locomotive Arms.

Despite his sharp wit, Guy was a nice chap, and he knew that we steam buffs accepted the compelling reasons for change. I reminded him that the sudden growth in railway preservation societies was strong evidence that the magic of steam was indestructible.

Steadily Guy Parkes moved up the managerial ladder and I saw less of him but, recalling our bet, I didn't forget in 1969 to call in his fourth-floor private office at Marylebone.

I knocked on his door and entered. He rose courteously from his chair and welcomed me warmly. 'Ah, Firebox Ferneyhough himself. Good to see you.' After an exchange of greetings and personal news, he asked, 'Come to pay your fiver, eh?'

'No, Guy. To collect.'

'How's that?'

'You've forgotten the Rheidol Valley line.'

It really took him aback. 'The Rheidol? Oh, blast and damnation! So I have!'

He reached for his wallet and handed me a £5 note. I held it but didn't particularly want to keep it. Then unwittingly he found me a way out. 'You're not going to believe this, Firebox, but I've joined the Severn Valley Railway Society.'

When I'd stopped laughing, I returned his fiver. 'For the society's funds with my compliments.'

'Oh, really? Thanks, old chap. D'you know, they let me drive a real loco for a hundred yards last autumn. And it was in full steam.'

I just couldn't help grinning at the fellow. 'You know, Guy, it gets you in the end.'

'I suppose so. By the way, you were quick off the mark.'

His new calendar for 1969 showed 1 January.

'Of course. We steam buffs like to be punctual.'

18
British Rail's Only Surviving Steam Line

Sharing my enthusiasm for steam, a colleague at the Railways Board HQ at Marylebone, my base, telephoned to say that he was working on the advance proofs for the spring timetable for 1969, the year after steam on British Rail had virtually ended, and had something special to show me. In two shakes of a shunter's pole I was in his office. He showed me a rough sheet headed, 'Aberystwyth and Devil's Bridge – Vale of Rheidol Railway – Operated by Steam Traction', and he had just checked the descriptive phrase, 'British Rail's only narrow-gauge Passenger Line passes through the magnificent scenery of the Rheidol Valley.' He also confirmed that this little railway was now the only steam-operated line owned and managed by British Rail.

In our metamorphosed railways of diesels and electrics, HSTs and APTs, the toytown Rheidol trains run on rails only 23½ inches apart, a spectacle to bring out the small boy in any man. They snort and struggle happily away from the popular coastal resort, climbing the wooded hills for nearly a dozen miles, to Devil's Bridge, 680 feet above sea-level, much as they have since 5 November 1902, the railway's opening day. Busy from spring to autumn, the railway brings a touch of magic for the youngsters and gives them some idea, in miniature, of what the real steam railways were like 'in the olden days' when mum and dad were children. One wonders how long this charming anachronism, this operating anomaly, in British Rail can survive. Each May I riffle anxiously through the new official timetable to see if it is still alive and steaming.

While on holiday with my wife recently, I sampled this very special ride and sniffed a whiff of steam drifting into the carriage through the open sides. Then we walked in the wooded hills near the quaint Devil's Bridge, revelling in the glorious scenery and enjoying a ploughman's lunch in a local hostelry.

At Devil's Bridge station, crowds gathered round the diminutive locomotive, sparkling in its livery of blue, with red buffer beams, black smokebox, squat dome and brass-rimmed chimney. We watched its manoeuvres from one of the trains to the other, ready for the return journey, and saw the enginemen fill the water-tanks from a real, splashing water column, turned on and off by a large handle – a sight once common, even on main lines. White puffs of steam whispered rhythmically from the chimney, to float away to nothingness in a vivid blue sky. Low in the hedgerows, frightened birds fluttered and scared rabbits scuttled.

Steep by railway standards, the last four miles are the toughest, at a gradient of 1 in 50, a climb which begins just past Aberffrwd station. Sitting there in the carriage, crowded with happy holiday-makers, the thrust can be felt as the engine gets to grips with this final challenge to its strength, and wheel flanges on the rails squeal with tension. It is a ride that proves to be an experience unique in steam railways, because of the sense of approaching climax as the train tops the rise and at last curves gracefully into the platform at Devil's Bridge station.

In the busiest months, three trains daily run double journeys. They will stop as required at the intermediate halts, which have delightful Welsh names – Llanbadarn, Glenrafon, Capel Bangor, Nantyronen, Aberffrwd, Rheidol Falls, and Rhiwfron.

How do you stop the train? It tells you in the BR timetable, in a style redolent of timetables of the last century: 'Passengers wishing to alight must give notice to the guard at the previous calling point. Passengers desiring to join must give an appropriate hand signal to the driver.' What can be more matey than that!

The locomotive that hauled our train was *Prince of Wales* No. 9. Built for the new railway in 1902 by Davies & Metcalfe of Romily near Manchester, it is the grand-daddy of them all. A sturdy 2-6-2 tank engine, its six coupled driving-wheels of thirty-inch diameter were designed to tackle the heavy gradients on this snaking line.

The other two locomotives – *Owain Glyndwr* No. 7 and *Llywelyn* No. 8 – were built by the Great Western Railway in Swindon Works in 1923. Since original building, all three engines have had much work done on them. In the 1970s they were rebuilt at Swindon, complete with rebuilt boilers, in major overhauls. From this, one may infer that some person in high authority believes there's plenty more work for them yet to do. Happy thought.

All three locomotives have been converted from coal-burning to oil, a system that generates a quick and fierce heat and needs careful handling, especially to prevent damage to firebars and firebox equipment. Fireboxes have been adapted as needed. Exteriors remain unchanged. Steam, of course, remains the power.

During that unusually dry and hot summer of 1976, the threat of lineside fires brought with it the cost of having the line patrolled by Forestry Commission staff. Spark-arresters had proved unreliable against red-hot ash being thrown from the locomotive chimneys; that was why the Commission suggested the conversion to oil.

Serving the passengers are sixteen carriages with bogies, and a four-wheeled guard's van. Four with open sides date back to 1923 and three, plus the guard's van, to 1937. Of the nine closed-in carriages, seven seat fifty-six passengers and two seat forty-eight. The standard British Rail blue livery matches the locomotives; lining is in white and black. They have grey roofs, brown under-carriages and pine interiors. A programme for refurbishing all sixteen carriages and the guard's van began in 1975, and all had had attention by 1981.

Over the years a mixed bag of rebuilt wagons has been bequeathed. The small fleet is now used almost entirely by the engineer's department for maintenance tasks, including some re-sleepering each year. Livery of the wagons is dove grey, the livery used on the Rheidol line before it was taken over by the Great Western Railway in 1923.

Signalling control consists of the staff-and-ticket system, with an intermediate 'block post' at Aberffrwd; communications are by Post Office telephone lines. In my stationmastering days I often met the staff-and-ticket system on single lines of railway, mainly in country areas. The staff, made of metal, serves as a key to unlock the signal, and a driver was not allowed to go forward into the section ahead without being given either the metal staff or, if another train was expected to follow in the same direction, a special ticket on which the signalman wrote brief details of the train.

Among the staff, for many years the oldest driver was William James who joined the railways in 1934.

At Aberystwyth station six art students at the University College of Wales, which stands high above the seaside town, spent a term in 1981 on a project that brings pleasure to many visitors. They constructed a huge mural which now graces the wall of the Rheidol line terminus platform.

Donated by the University, it depicts scenes of the resort and the Rheidol Valley, all linked to the steam railway. H. & R. Johnson, a Stoke-on-Trent firm, donated the tiles, so making the project possible. In recognition of the students' work, British Rail gave each a first-class rail ticket for a journey of their choice anywhere in Britain.

Hard to believe now, the line cost £67,900 to build in 1901-2. Another surprise is that the contractors had difficulty in finding local labour. But the problem was solved with the completion of the Elan Valley reservoirs, which dammed up the water and released an avalanche of navvies onto the hitherto peaceful Rheidol Valley.

Tourists rushed to ride on the new trains. Scenically, the journey by a railway was far better than by road, and the trains were much more comfortable than the horse-drawn coach bumping along on the rough, hilly roads of the time. Soon, the coach was put out of business.

Shortly after the motor age arrived, a motor charabanc met some trains at Devil's Bridge to take climbers and walkers to a good starting point, and in the evenings it ferried the devout to revivalist meetings at the chapels up the valley. Mine-owners found the goods trains valuable for sending ore to Aberystwyth or beyond for smelting. In 1913 the company was taken over by the Cambrian Railway. But by that time the mining business was failing, and the threat of World War I made affairs worse. In the great railway amalgamations of 1923, the little line snuggled up cosily to its new parent, the Great Western.

On taking over, the GWR scrapped two of the three original locomotives and built two more mentioned earlier. These two 2-6-2 tanks were more powerful than the earlier one, with a tractive effort of 10,510 lb. They acquired their names – *Owain Glyndwr* and *Llywelyn* – in 1956. Over sixty years and still going strong!

Throughout its life, the little railway has had its ups and downs. You can still see the remains of mine shafts that once kept the line busy, with their rich deposits of lead and zinc and modest amounts of silver: shafts that today intrigue the industrial archaeologist. The once-flourishing mining hamlets are almost ghost villages, disturbed and enlivened only by the flutterings and scamperings of the local wildlife and by visitors who enjoy exploring the countryside.

Only the enormous interest of passengers, anxious to ride vintage steam, has kept the line alive. After British Rail got rid of steam in 1968, further interest developed. Then, in 1970, a voluntary society was formed, with a name nearly as long as the line itself – 'The Vale of Rheidol Railway Supporters' Association', VoRRSA for short. This, too, is unique. Its aims are to retain and develop a line owned by British Rail; in turn, BR plays an official and active part in the association's affairs. In railway societies, this is rare. BR publish an attractive illustrated brochure containing an application form for membership. For a modest annual fee, members are kept informed about the services and developments. Members are spread far and wide – in Britain and Europe, Canada and America. New members, including people with children, join each year, especially after a journey on the line and a visit to the British Rail souvenir shop at Devil's Bridge.

At the initiative of BR, the Rheidol route is promoted by a joint marketing panel along with two other famous narrow-gauge lines – the Festiniog and the Talyllin, both owned and run by voluntary societies.

One of the special charms of the Rheidol, I noticed, was that, because of the frequent curves, the steaming locomotive keeps coming into view to passengers seated at either side of the carriages. When a puff of steam blew into the face of the little boy sitting next to me, he grimaced and made a noise like 'yuk!' But his father grinned, exhorting him, 'It's a beautiful smell, me boy!'

19

In Trouble with the Railway Police

On the railway we had our own police force. It was quite separate from the civil police, but both forces co-operated. Now, let me tell you about a few police cases of the several I came across. One of them dates back to the time when I was based at Hasland near Chesterfield as a relief stationmaster. I was there for several weeks, my staff consisting of clerks, shunters, yard foremen and signalmen. The title of my job was yardmaster.

The first I heard of the thieving from goods vans, which was taking place at the dead of night in our marshalling sidings, was when yard foreman Tim Coleby came to see me. To talk privately, we stood outside the ancient brick office which I shared with the three clerks. We were about fifty yards from the main line of four tracks running between Nottingham and Chesterfield and close by the Hasland locomotive sheds. Steam and smoke hung heavy in the still air. Expresses and heavy goods trains were constantly steaming up and down the main tracks.

Tim Coleby, fiftyish, a good worker, was popular with his men. His clean-shaven face was pallid and deeply lined, as found in many who have spent most of their working lives on shifts.

Today the lines were deeper than usual. 'I've got a complaint, Mr Ferney. The police is in the sidings, two of 'em. Plain clothes. And they're harassing me something terrible. I don't think I can stand much more. And I'm innocent.'

It was not news to me that our railway police were around. Still, they're bound to work in secrecy, I suppose. I looked at Tim's drawn face. 'Tell me, what's the trouble?'

'They say there's been thieving at night. From goods vans in the sidings.'

'But you've said you're innocent.'

He had rolled a cigarette. As he lit it, a quarter of it burned

198

away, the tobacco being a litle sparse. He inhaled deeply. 'Yes, a-course I'm innocent. But you try telling them coppers that!'
'Now look, Tim. If you're innocent you've nothing to fear.'
'Yes, but some of the lads who are suspected have been saying that I knowed about it. Anyways, that's what the police says. They could be bluffing. To trap me. And they says as I was in charge, I ought to know what my men is doing.' Then he appealed, 'Mr Ferney, can you stop 'em from harassing me, please?'
It would be risky for me to make snap judgements about men like Tim whom I had worked with for only a few weeks. He might be a real rogue for all I knew.
'I've every sympathy, Tim, but I don't think there's anything I can do. I could say that so far I have always found you trustworthy.'
'That's summat, anyroad.' He lifted his cap, scratched his thinning dark hair and looked across towards the main line as a London-bound express hurtled along the track, belching steam and smoke. 'You know, sir, it's really making me ill. Reckon I oughta go on the sicklist.'
'Would that be wise? It could raise suspicions.'
Dejected, he muttered, 'I suppose so. I just can't see no way out.'
'Now look, old chap. Go back to the sidings and do your job as usual. Don't discuss it with anybody. Just keep yourself busy and concentrate on what you're doing. If you're innocent, you've nothing to fear. But I'm afraid I can't interfere with police enquiries as long as they are reasonable with you. Come and talk to me again. Any time.'
'Ta, sir. I'll do that.'
He walked off, shoulders sagging. No doubt he was worrying about his wife and three children.
Later a police detective called on me. I was able to go outside without arousing too much interest among the clerks.
He began, 'We've got a problem, guv'nor.'
'Oh, what's that?'
'A few nights ago, two of us travelled inside a van of mixed goods. We got in at Nottingham. Our sixth trip in a month. About three that morning, it stood in your sidings.'

'Here, at Hasland?'

He was in plain clothes and seemed to be a kindly man. Smartish fellow. I guessed him to be in his mid-thirties, not much older than me. I decided not to volunteer anything but just to answer his questions.

'Yes,' he said, 'here at Hasland. The sliding door was opened, very quietly. About two feet. We were hiding behind a couple of bales and we could just see in the darkness two chaps climb in. We watched while they rummaged through the parcels. One of them threw a large package out of the van onto the ground." I waited for more. 'So we tackled them in the light of a flashlamp and grabbed one. The other jumped and got away. The lad we caught was only about twenty. He was real scared and wouldn't name his mate. But he kept on saying, "It's not only me. It's me mates, them shunters".' He looked at his wristwatch. 'I'll come and see you again shortly. There's more enquiries to make.'

'I'll have to send a report to my district officer. All right with you?'

'Sure. We want to keep things quiet awhile. Can you make it brief and mark it personal?'

'Yes, I'll do that.'

He was back on the Monday. 'Court case at Chesterfield on Saturday. We called on two or three homes and found shoes, chocolates and cigarettes. It's taken six months to crack this one. We felt sure at first that it was an inside job. But we were wrong. Not a single railwayman was involved.'

'That's a great relief. Thanks.'

On the Saturday morning I attended the court as an 'official railway observer', or, to put it less technically, as a nosey parker. My presence was neither necessary nor invited. I just wanted to know who, why and the size of the sentences, if any.

As I sat in the court, three miscreants stood before the magistrates on the bench. Police evidence was given, and all the rigmarole of the court procedure was processed, most of it unfamiliar to me. My knowledge of the English court procedure was limited to scenes in crime films. However, I was pleased to have it confirmed that none of the men at Hasland was involved. The lad who had referred to 'shunters' had thrown unnecessary suspicion on my men.

An experience concerning police dogs interested me immensely. In the 1950s, I was the assistant editor of the British Railways staff magazine, a recent promotion, and I was writing a feature article which, during provincial visits to railway police centres, had taken me to Hull. But I never knew that the story I was seeking would reveal a touching tragedy.

On arrival at Hull station, I was met by police sergeant Walter Bloss, for many years a police dog trainer. He explained about the work in his division and motored me to the dog compound several miles away in the country. Out through the suburbs and into a bucolic setting of farms and meadows, the sergeant chatted away, recounting fascinating yarns about his work. On arrival, we visited the kennels which house some of the most beautiful, innocent-looking Alsatian dogs I had ever seen, but I was not allowed too close to them. One or two began to bark, obviously having sniffed out and espied a stranger. I found my small talk drying up.

Now I saw a constable coming along the footpath on which we were standing. I had the feeling in my bones that this was a set-up. Knowing what jokers some railwaymen could be, I suspected that the police might come up with stronger stuff. Walking towards us, the constable was certainly a handler, for at the end of his strong leather lead was a really enormous Alsatian. It wore no muzzle and couldn't have looked more friendly. Having had experience only of pet canines, I could hardly claim to be a percipient doggie man.

As the animal came closer, he began to bark. Dogs, they say, can tell when you are frightened. They can smell the fear that oozes from your pores as you perspire. Man and dog stood a few yards from the sergeant and me. Greetings and introductions were politely exchanged, interspersed by a modicum of meaningless smalltalk and forced laughter. Reaching for his wallet, the sergeant took out a £5 note and held it out towards me. I had no idea what he was up to, but I found my knees were very slightly trembling.

'Mr Ferneyhough,' the sergeant said firmly, 'Here's a fiver. Grab it out of my hand and the money is yours.'

So this was it. 'What'll happen if I do?'

'Why not try it and see?'

'But I'll get bitten.'

He was persuasive. 'Not at all. We'll see to that. There's nothing to be afraid of.'

Putting on a face of bravado, I said smartly, 'Not bloody likely! I don't want my arm bitten off!'

Both the men laughed, and the handler quietened the dog.

The sergeant told me, 'If you'd been a stranger and had made a grab for the fiver, that dog would have had your arm between his teeth before you even touched it!'

'Now he tells me! Come on, Sergeant. I think I've seen enough for the moment.'

He and I walked back to his car and he assured me, 'Only a bit of fun. You were as safe as houses.'

On the way back to Hull, he filled me in with more details about the work of the dogs and I made rough notes for the article I was preparing. Dogs were found to be very useful patrolling the docks with a handler. He said they were being used more frequently also to keep in order unruly football fans travelling by special train to support their home teams in 'away' games.

Sergeant Bloss told me that he had always loved dogs and had been a trainer in the British Railways Police for a dozen years. There was no other job he would rather do. He had mastered the techniques and knew he was good in his tasks. Most of us enjoy the work we can do well.

At the extensive docks at Hull, temptations were strong for the thieving fraternity, and the dogs proved a powerful deterrent. Most criminals were afraid of large dogs, especially Alsatians. Sergeant Bloss described an incident when he was patrolling the docks with a dog, on night duty. In a large warehouse during the small hours he spotted a moving shadow behind some packing cases. He checked the security of the dog's muzzle, slipped his leash, then whispered, 'Find him, Bruce!' Moving silently forward, the dog quickly cornered the man, who was soon screaming in stark terror. The dog jumped up at him, but it was impossible for the animal to bite his victim, who, in his fright, might not have realized that the dog was muzzled. The sergeant said, 'I slipped the cuffs on the fellow, and within an hour he was in the lock-up.'

An incident the sergeant described to me on the way back to Hull was enough to curdle the blood:

'I was taking an Alsatian from the compound back to Hull one morning. Named Rover. He wasn't muzzled. I think I made a mistake there, but I knew this four-year-old so well. A beautiful fellow. Really playful. I'd brought him up from a puppy and we were great friends. I just loved that dog.'

He slowed down a bit. Approaching the town, the traffic became more congested. 'You know how the docks come right into the city? Well, the siren of an enormous ship startled Rover. He was sitting with me on the back seat and he began to bark. The siren sounded again. That really set him off. He was real agitated. Constable Mike Tremlett was driving and he asked if we should stop. But I told him to keep driving. Steadily.

'Then a railway engine in the sidings gave a loud whistle. That did it. Rover went berserk. He frothed at the mouth. I tried to quieten him. But he went for me. He bit my wrist and fetched blood. The pain was pretty nasty, and I realized I just had to master him.

'Mike was busy keeping an eye on the traffic and slowed down. I don't think he realized how nasty my position was. But I was too scared to talk.

'Then the dog suddenly jumped on top of me and was going for my neck. I grabbed him by the throat and I felt his hot breath on my face. Oh, God, I thought. It's him or me for it. A fight to a finish. I pressed my fingers deeper into his throat. Heavens, how he fought! My body was wet with sweat. I was sure I was going under.'

He slowed down in the congested traffic and continued. 'My fingers were numb and my throat was parched. But I just had to hold on. I was putting all my physical power into my fingers. And I held and held. I felt the car stop. Rover slowly went limp and quiet as he slid to the floor.'

Keeping one hand on the steering-wheel, the sergeant reached for his handkerchief and dabbed his forehead. 'Mr Ferneyhough, it was the most terrible experience of my life. I didn't sleep properly for weeks. There was an enquiry, of course. Our chief constable took it. But everybody was very sympathetic.'

We were now approaching Hull station. 'The chief offered to transfer me to another post. He'd let me choose. But I told him I couldn't leave the dogs. They were my life. The old man patted me on the shoulder and said, "Good fellow!" '

My day at Hull with the police dogs was over. I had planned to write up my notes on the return train to London, but I couldn't write a word. My mind was so full of all the details of the day. The moment I specially remember was when Sergeant Bloss saw me off on my train at Hull. He shook me vigorously by the hand and said, 'It's been real good to talk to you.' And I noticed there were tears in his eyes.

By the time I had another assignment for a police feature, I had been promoted to executive editor of our staff magazine, taking charge of a small team. Another promotion I was to receive later would require me to write speeches for Railways Board chairmen, including the highly controversial Dr Beeching. But that's another story.

Back to the police. My appointment was with the top policeman of the lot, the chief constable himself. He was based at BR headquarters at Marylebone. My brief was to write an article describing the structure of the railway police, from local offices through district and divisional areas to the top policy authority.

I had already completed my researches in the field – from the security of local railway premises and property and various installations to investigating missing luggage and fare-dodging. I described their court work, liaison with civil police, power of arrest, control of crowds at stations and on trains for special public and sporting occasions, local and national. Right down to restoring lost children to their anxious parents and helping dear grandma find her missing luggage.

Now I sought policy angles. I would later submit my draft article to the chief constable for his formal approval. This was normal routine for articles about the various railway departments.

Being a little early for my interview, I stood in the corridor outside the secretary's office. Shortly, out came a passenger guard carrying his uniform cap and dabbing a handkerchief to his eyes. I was surprised to recognize the man, Alf Barnes. I had met him often on the Paddington-Exeter-Penzance route. Always smart, always with highly polished shoes and invariably sporting a flower in his lapel.

Foolishly, perhaps, I spoke to him. 'Alf, what's the matter, old chap?'

But he only muttered into his handkerchief and stumbled off towards the lift. It must be something serious, I thought, as I entered the secretary's office. I was ushered into The Presence. The chief constable's private room was quietly furnished. On the wall hung a pendulum clock with a slow tick. But what captured me most was the collection of the heterogeneous accoutrements of police life displayed in a glass-fronted showcase, designed in mahogany marquetry: a pair of crude iron handcuffs, an ancient police whistle, old leather truncheon, top hat, lantern, Victorian notebook and pair of leather boots were the main contents.

The chief constable was a fatherly-looking man with a good head of greying hair and military-style moustache, and attired in a quiet navy-blue serge suit. He greeted me courteously. We had met before, briefly, on several occasions.

I said, 'What a splendid picture. May I look at it, please?'

'Of course.'

On the mantelpiece was a large sepia photograph of a scene I remembered from 1937. That year the LMS had celebrated the hundredth anniversary of the opening of the London & Birmingham Railway, its pioneering trunk line. There at Euston station stood the handsome young detective superintendent with Sir Josiah Stamp, chairman of the LMS, and other dignitaries. Behind them was *Cornwall*, the fine 2-2-2 locomotive, still one of the oldest working steam-locomotives in the world, built at Crewe in 1847 by Francis Trevithick, son of the great Richard. When, in my twenties, I had visited the exhibition at Euston in 1937, the most striking feature to me was that her two driving wheels at eight feet six inches in diameter were higher than the ceiling in a modern suburban house.

As we got down to business, I filled a few pages of my notebook with the untidy Pitman's shorthand which even I found hard to decipher if I delayed the transcription too long.

When we were finished, I noticed that the chief constable was in a relaxed and expansive mood, and I was simply bursting with curiosity about guard Alf Barnes. Without any lead from me, the chief began to talk about the man, unaware that I knew him.

'I've just had a sad case to deal with, Ferneyhough,' he confided. 'A passenger guard with an excellent record helping a couple of thieves to rifle mailbags on an express West Country train.' He shook his head. 'Very sad. Very sad indeed. A family man, not yet fifty. Such a fool. I've had him in my office. You might have passed him in the corridor. Did you see him?'

I didn't particularly want to admit it, but how can you possibly tell a lie to the top copper of British Railways? And in his own private office, too.

'Well, yes. I did spot a man in uniform. Just briefly.'

'I had to warn him it might be a case for the courts, and he simply broke down and wept.'

'Poor chap. I'm sorry for him.'

'I couldn't console the fellow. And he suddenly blurted out, "If I had a gun I'd shoot meself!" Quick as a flash, I opened my top drawer, whipped out my revolver and banged it down on the desk in front of him. "There you are," I said. "Have a go!" '

'My goodness!'

'He groaned and pushed the gun away and covered his face with both hands. He kept muttering, "Take it away, Guv'nor. Take it away!" '

The chief's tactic shocked me and I suggested tentatively, 'Wasn't that – er, just a little drastic, sir?'

'No, not really. It would bring him to his senses. I've dealt with many like him in my time.' He grinned wryly.

'I don't suppose the gun was loaded?'

'Good heavens, of course not. But the guard wouldn't know that. Without going into details, our enquiries revealed that he was being blackmailed. Most unfortunate. I don't want to see a good man sacked and his career finished. And we have a good chance of finding a way out for him.'

He loaded his pipe, and when he had filled the air with the strong aroma of tobacco, he told me another story. 'This one dates back to my days on the LMS when I was chief super. I was travelling back from Glasgow first class and I had dinner and half a bottle of wine on the train. I was unknown to the dining-car staff, and the chief steward gave me a used receipt. It took a sharp eye to rumble it, but I've seen many like it.'

I chuckled. 'He could have kicked himself had he known!'

'You bet. I gave him a fat tip when paying the bill.'

'Why was that?'

'Just to lead the fellow on. Stop him from becoming suspicious.'

'Oh, I see. Of course.'

'I said nothing to him on the train. In fact, I treated him with the greatest courtesy. Later we had no problem in tracking him down. We found the whole team were on the fiddle. Eventually they were all sacked.

'Several months earlier one of that team had had a personal interview with Arthur Towle, head of LMS hotels, and asked for a transfer to a hotel. Mr Towle pressed him for his reasons, which he suspected anyway. An honest man caught up in a web of intrigue. The fellow wouldn't budge from saying that all he wanted was a change from travelling. He was given a job at the Welcome Hotel at Stratford-on-Avon. If he had stayed on the trains, he would probably have been sacked with the others.'

He smiled as though at other recollections. 'In my days on the LMS in the 1930s, the chief travelling auditor was given a dud receipt. Just imagine! He'd had dinner on the train from Sheffield to St Pancras. That chief steward also got the sack. The auditor and I had fun comparing notes. Those two stewards couldn't have chosen two more deserving victims!'

When, a week later, I called on the chief constable about my article, I was delighted that he approved it, almost as it was, for print. As I rose to leave his office, he commented, 'You might be glad to hear about that guard.'

'I would indeed, sir.'

'As I said, there was a blackmailing element, and we managed to get him exonerated in court. He's had his lesson and is now back on the Exeter expresses.'

'I'm very glad. Thank you for telling me.'

20
The Man Who Hated his Fame

Now for a few thoughts about the Beeching Plan and Beeching the man.

Dr Richard Beeching (Baron, 1965) at the age of forty-seven was appointed chairman of the British Transport Commission 1961-3 and of the British Railways Board 1963-5. His credentials? ARCS, BSc, DIC, PhD, CI MechE, AIM, FInstP, MInstT – surely adequate qualifications to sort out the railways. His stint was expected to run for five years. Instead, it was four. A change of government took place in October 1964 from Conservative to Labour. He did not stay long after that. No prizes for guessing why.

In the Railways Board annual report for 1962 which Dr Beeching presented to the Minister of Transport, it was noted: 'During the past fifteen years they had witnessed a dramatic decline in the fortunes of many railways throughout the world, and British Railways was no exception.'

Because of mounting financial difficulties, Beeching was expected to bring radical changes in policy and management. A formidable task. On his appointment and right until he left, he received massive and continuous personal publicity. Much was directed to his fantastically high salary of £24,000 (the rate he was paid as a former director of ICI), compared with that of his predecessor, Sir Brian Robertson, of £10,000. Popular newspapers lavished us with their special skills with relish. 'Dr Beeching, £24,000 Rail Boss, closes another wayside station ...' or 'Dr Beeching, £24,000 Rail Chief, scratches his nose on Glasgow Central station. Is this a secret sign in code denoting more closures in Scotland?' But the agile cyclist and Minister of Transport Ernest Marples, who sponsored Beeching, explained that taxes would take all of this excepting £6,500. Enough, one hoped, to keep his home in East Grinstead, Sussex, financially viable.

How original was the Minister's *coup* in capturing this ICI gem? In 1926 Sir Guy Granet, LMS chairman 1924-7, had snaffled an earlier director of the ICI board. This other brilliant performer, Sir Josiah Stamp, was to become the top man of the LMS. Stamp held the position for fifteen years. Beeching lasted only four. Legitimate question: did Marples know about Stamp?

Incidentally, Beeching was in the midst of the great change-over from steam trains to diesels and electrics. That decision was made in 1955. Then, it was forecast by the Board that the next fifteen years would witness the greatest revolution ever seen in modern times on any railway in the world. Eventually it would put Britain in the lead in wheel-to-rail transport.

In his vision of the future, Beeching reminded people that, 'Our steam railways were developed to their fullest extent at a time when the horse and cart was the only means of feeding to and distributing from them.' (Two years after Beeching arrived on the scene, British Railways still had dozens of horses on their books. It is not known whether anyone had the courage to tell the great doctor this.)

Looking ahead, Beeching claimed that British Railways should concentrate on the sort of work they were good at – the mass movement of people and goods, and leave other kinds of transport to services more fitted to it, such as door-to-door movements performed by cars, coaches and motor lorries.

In his reshaping plan, which was based on extensive researches, he produced some devastating facts:

Stopping passenger trains were by far the worst loss-makers in the passenger business.

One third of the route mileage carried only about one twentieth of the total passenger business.

One half of the total route mileage carried only about one twentieth of the total freight-mile tons.

Operating losses were likely to go on increasing unless radical changes were made.

Before Beeching could close a passenger station or branch line, rigorous procedures had to be processed. Hurdles included the Transport Consultative Committees, other interested authorities and the Minister of Transport. So, in fact, Beeching alone did not, could not, close passenger stations or branch lines. He made proposals. The Minister took the decision.

Beeching said, 'The railways will never pay unless we do some quite drastic pruning. What is required is a real surgical operation. The Cabinet must publicly accept responsibility for the future of thousands of miles of track than can never be made to pay.' By using a medical metaphor, he gave the newspapers the chance to talk about 'the good Doctor'. Many readers could be forgiven for thinking that Beeching *was* a medical doctor.

Beeching fans believed that the most vociferous objectors to his proposed closures often came from people who rarely used the trains. They just liked the idea of their own little village station and the branch line. They liked to go down to the station in the family car on a sunny afternoon with the children to see those dear, sweet little trains go chugging by under a delightful plume of dazzling white steam. And it was a bonus to hear the engine whistle scream.

On the freight side, Beeching's reorganization increased the average speeds and lengthened the through journeys of freight trains, which helped to get rid of surplus marshalling yards. In the year he started, there were 867 marshalling yards in use, and in the year he finished 378. He pushed ahead with the vast modernization programme and gave new impetus in the field of marketing.

In the year he started, there were 7,025 passenger and goods stations open, and in the year he left 4,295. By 1970, after his departure – the Labour Party was in power 1964-70, the number had been reduced further to 2,868, which, to those on the inside, tells its own story.

Like his many predecessors, Beeching had been unable to make the railways pay, but undoubtedly he cut their annual losses handsomely, with appropriate savings to the taxpayer. He reduced the deficit by £35 million and increased the productivity of British Railways by about twenty-five per cent. He brought in many developments and improvements, injected new blood into middle and top management to fertilize new ideas and applied fresh thoughts to stale problems.

Much of this basic information I used in the notes I wrote for Beeching's public speeches and in the talks I myself gave up and down the country to Rotary, universities, Lions International, local political branches and other 'opinion-forming bodies', all of which brought much excitement and a modicum of fun and laughter.

When he left, the railways were in the dying throes of the age of steam, steam making its last despairing gasp, steam which had been invented by the great British pioneers, steam which had been cradled in Britain and had begun the railway concept world-wide, steam with all its magic and wonder and mystery that lives in the dedicated hands of the railway preservation societies and their enthusiastic supporters. I was at British Railways headquarters long before Beeching arrived, and I was still there long after he had gone. Personalities come and go, but the railways, it seems, go on for ever.

One day, when Beeching was travelling somewhere, I happened to call on Marjorie, his temporary secretary, on the richly carpeted first floor at Marylebone HQ. I said to her, 'Do you mind if I go into the inner sanctum and try his chair for size?'

She giggled, appraised my medium-sized dimensions and no doubt compared them with Beeching's bulk. 'Help yourself. It should be a sight for sore eyes!'

I tapped gently on the great man's door. It didn't seem decent just to walk in boldly, even if his office was empty. Solemnly I sat in the doctor's deep, well-upholstered chair at his great, polished mahogany desk. This, I noticed, was absolutely clear of all paperwork. That shows a great man. Always a clear desk. He can then spend all his free time delegating, telling others what work to do. In the chair I sat back in a leisurely manner, felt a surge of power coursing through my veins and grabbed fiercely at the telephone to call Marjorie. She answered in a most seductive voice.

'Chairman's secretary, sir. Can I do something for you, sir?'
I bawled into the mouthpiece. 'Get me the Minister. And
make it snappy!'

'Idiot!' she said, laughing. Then, suddenly, a note of
urgency in her voice as she whispered hoarsely, 'Oh, God!
He's just coming in. Quick!'

She banged the telephone down. You could have knocked
me down with a rail chair. Just as I replaced the telephone, in
walked Dr B. I felt the surge of power coursing in reverse
rapidly through my veins.

The great man gave me the gentlest of faint smiles. 'May I
sit down?'

Never have I catapulted out of a chair so fast. I muttered,
'Sorry, sir. I do beg your pardon, sir!'

As befits a great man, he totally ignored me. He sat down
in his chair, no doubt still warm, and contemplated his
absolutely clear desk.

As I skedaddled through Marjorie's room, she looked up
at the ceiling and shrugged.

On the way back to my room, I recalled that he had been
at our headquarters for about three years. Almost certainly
he did not know me, even though I had attended several of
his Press conferences in the board-room. I wanted to say to
him, 'Look, sir, I'm the anonymous guy who's been writing
your speech notes these past three years, sir. I'm also the guy
who travels up and down Britain giving public talks about
your Great Plan for the railways, the Beeching Plan, sir. In
this sort of work, I get all sorts of rough deals. I've never had
tomatoes thrown at me, nor been spat upon. And I've never
been kicked in the Gorbals, as you were by a trade union
man down Glasgow way. But people chuck other brutal filth
at me, like – why are your fares so high and your trains
always so late? Why have you closed our wayside halt?
Why is your salary so high? Do you know, sir, I'm just a big
punchbag, a receptacle for boring insults intended for *you*.

'Let me tell you, sir, in the local town hall the other
evening, a fellow had the cheek to accuse me of being just a
post office for the views of Dr Beeching, and said that you,
sir, were just a post office for the views of the Minister of

Transport, and that the Minister was just a post office for the views of the government.

'Sir, I had to say to the guy that he and other voters like him had voted the government into power, who had appointed the Minister, who had appointed Dr Beeching. So I told this guy that it was him and voters of his kind who are responsible for all the so-called Beeching closures and not Dr Beeching. And that quietened him, sir, but not for long.'

Since writing these notes, I learnt that Dr Richard (then Lord) Beeching had died, aged seventy-one. It was in March 1985. He once said that he resented his 'axeman' reputation, and complained, with a gentle smile, that it was 'an injustice I shall suffer in history'. Another notable phrase is, 'All I cut off were twigs with no sap in them.' In a television interview in 1981 he said that he had no misgivings about his railway plans of the 1960s but felt some regret that they were not pursued with the necessary vigour.

Beeching spent less time at the top than any other chairman of British Railways since World War II but made a far greater impact than any of them. His place in history is assured, though perhaps not quite as he would have wished. He was a relaxed and pleasant man, easy to talk to and with a friendly smile.*

* A fuller and more serious account of Dr Beeching's work for British Railways appears in my book *The History of Railways in Britain*, Osprey, 1975.

21
How Permanent is the BR Permanent Way?

Have you ever wondered just how permanent is the 'permanent way' of our railways? To the Victorians, railways must have seemed indestructible. When Queen Victoria, aged twenty-three, risked her first ride on a steam train from Slough, near Windsor, to Paddington in 1842, less than 2,000 route miles had been laid in Britain. When she died, in 1901, the permanent way had reached nearly 19,000 miles. Then, from 1940, it began to diminish from its peak of about 20,000 to around the current 10,000-plus. Clearly, not so permanent after all.

Today technical innovation increases the pace of change. Daily we meet new gadgets and unfamiliar methods and styles. Many features in our lives, which we have come to know well and to have affection for, are slipping away. The firm foundations of our permanent way are being disturbed. Our propensity to hang on to the past is probably why most of us are hoarders. To throw away some useless piece from the past is almost like discarding a tiny part of our very selves. The style of our daily life changes so fast that we tend to compensate by clinging to the old and familiar.

It is now highly fashionable to cultivate nostalgic pursuits. One of these involves the five hundred railway preservation societies that do so much to keep alive the interest in steam. Surprisingly, among the two million railway enthusiasts are many young people. Though some are too young to remember the romantic days of steam, steam running, now a novelty, is a main preoccupation and there are over twenty private railways for them to choose from in England, Wales and Scotland.

The loss of something 'permanent' from my young life hit me at the age of seventeen. From Hanley station, where I

worked, we could see the electric trams passing by, driven
from overhead wires. They whined up and down the steep
road from morning till night. The warning bell, clanged by the
driver's foot, and the squeal of wheels on iron rails at curves
were familiar and friendly sounds. On family visits to friends
and relations, we children loved to scramble up the steep
iron staircase for seats on the swaying upper deck. The trams
had taken much business from the local railway line. Yet
eventually the trams were silenced by the faster and more
manoeuvrable motor buses. And after 11 July 1928 people in
the Potteries saw and heard their electric trams no more.

That day I felt more than a little sadness at the loss of this
familiar transport. Something fundamental had vanished
from my youthful daily scene for ever. But the railways, ah –
the railways! Their permanent way, I was sure, would remain
for ever and ever: a comforting thought, especially as I was
due one day to join the pension fund!

Yet, locked away in an arcane future, another sad story
awaited me. A gentleman named Dr Richard Beeching was, in
the 1960s, to close the Hanley loop line along with many
more, under force of circumstance. Later still, the track which
I had known as the *permanent* way would be taken up and the
steel rails sold for scrap. Finally, Hanley station, where I
started my railway life, scene of many happy hours, would be
torn down to make way for a carpark to suit people whose
lives would be geared more to the motor car.

Today, looking ahead at the permanent way, the total route
mileage of 10,000-plus is unlikely to be reduced much more
for at least several decades. One can only judge by the vast
amount of capital resources now invested for further developments, such as more main-line electrification and new
trains. Overseas, too, especially in the under-developed coun-
tries where much steam operation is still to be seen, massive
investments in railways are continuing.

Our own railways, I conjecture, are not absolutely permanent, but they are certainly here to serve Britain well into
the twenty-first century and are, I submit, guaranteed to
sustain the traditional love/hate relationship with the great
travelling public.

Index

Index

219